"As you live the Christian life,
you may have periods
of darkness or of doubt.
You may encounter painful struggles
and discouragement.
But there will also be moments
of exultation and glory.
And most important of all,
you will become free."

IVP
CLASSICS

The Fight

A Practical Handbook for Christian Living

ABRIDGED EDITION

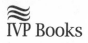

JOHN WHITE

FOREWORD BY BILL HYBELS

IVP Books

An imprint of InterVarsity Press
Downers Grove, Illinois

InterVarsity Press
P.O. Box 1400, Downers Grove, IL 60515-1426
World Wide Web: www.ivpress.com
E-mail: email@ivpress.com

InterVarsity Press® is the book-publishing division of InterVarsity Christian Fellowship/USA®, a student movement active on campus at hundreds of universities, colleges and schools of nursing in the United States of America, and a member movement of the International Fellowship of Evangelical Students. For information about local and regional activities, write Public Relations Dept., InterVarsity Christian Fellowship/USA, 6400 Schroeder Rd., P.O. Box 7895, Madison, WI 53707-7895, or visit the IVCF website at <www.intervarsity.org>.

Design: Cindy Kiple

Images: Malcolm Fire/ Getty Images

ISBN 978-0-8308-3409-9

Printed in the United States of America ∞

Library of Congress Cataloging-in-Publication Data

White, John, 1924 Mar. 5-2002.
    The fight: a practical handbook for Christian living / John White.
        p. cm.
    Originally published: Downers Grove, Ill.: InterVarsity Press
    c1976. Includes bibliographical references. ISBN 978-0-8308-3409-9
    (pbk.: alk. paper)
    1. Christian life. I. Title.
    BV4501.3.W46625 2007
    248.4—dc22

                                                                    2007031475

P	16	15	14	13	12	11	10	9	8	7	6	5	4	3	2	1
Y	20	19	18	17	16	15	14	13	12	11	10	09	08	07			

To Alec Clifford

without whose encouragement I would

never have written for publication

Contents

Foreword

———— 🦅 ————

Early on in my ministry someone gave me a book called *The Fight* by John White. It was so important to me at the time. It presented Christianity as worth the struggle. That spiritual growth was worth the *fight* for it.

The Fight explained how there was a cosmic battle going on between the activity of God in the world and the activity of the evil one in the world. It helped me understand how those forces are in opposition to each other and where I fit in to that whole cosmic battle.

I probably read that book four or five times. I preached from significant portions of it and did some sermon series out of it. I owe a lot to John White and InterVarsity Press for that book.

I am happy to commend this IVP Classics edition of *The Fight* and pray that a new generation of readers will benefit from it the way I did.

Bill Hybels
Senior Pastor, Willow Creek Community Church

1

Beginnings

———— ✦ ————

When you became a Christian, a number of extremely important events took place both in heaven and in your own body.

You may or may not have felt anything. Christians have widely differing experiences, ranging from intense emotions to nothing at all. You may not even be able to say when you became a Christian. All you may know is that at that moment you acknowledged the Jesus of history to be your Savior and your God.

Yet whatever you did or did not feel and whether or not you know when you became a Christian, the events I speak of took place. As I describe them I shall, in a way, be defining what a Christian is.

Purely psychological events occur in all varieties of conversion. Had you been converted to communism or to any religion or worldview, you would have experienced them. The psychological factors have been long recognized and well described. They consist of temporary "feeling states" and a turn around in a person's understanding of life.

In Christian conversion, as in any other conversion, you may experience many such psychological events, and you will certainly experience a change in life view. What makes Christian conversion different is that supernatural events also occur. The feeling states in non-Christian conversion are temporary. They are equally temporary in Christian conversion. But the supernatural, and often unfelt, events are permanent. They mark you in the sight of demons and angels as a human who is different. They bring your body into touch with eternity and with the eternal God.

A NEW STATUS BEFORE GOD

In the first place, you have been *justified*. This is to say that God looks upon you and deals with you as *though you were perfectly righteous*, as though you had never sinned and will never sin. However difficult this idea may be for you to grasp, it represents an event that has already taken place and will never change.

It is not that God wears blinders and pretends you are better than you are. He knows about your sin. Yet his feelings toward you and his dealings with you are based on a righteousness Christ has given you. God treats you as though you were as righteous as Jesus. You may be uncomfortable with this idea, but as the impact of it breaks over your understanding you will marvel. Far from wanting to sin you will sense how you have been set free to be holy.

Your justification is both a heavenly event and a time-space event. It is a heavenly event insofar as Jesus is at this moment on the right hand of God's throne acting as your personal representative. It is a heavenly event too in that your name is now recorded in the "not guilty" annals of heaven. It is an earthly event since you, a creature of time and space, may boldly step into the presence of the God of eternity and hold a conversation with him. Indeed you are encouraged to do so. Notice, you are not given permission to *crawl* into God's presence but to approach him with your head held high.

A second event that took place in your body is what is known as *regeneration* or new birth. Eternity invaded space and reestablished permanent links between your personality and the Eternal. Again, you may have experienced little or nothing when this most profound event occurred. By a miracle of divine grace a nonbiological life was implanted in you. It is a form of life that will enable you one day to inhabit eternity just as your biological life now enables you to live in time-space.

The life that entered you was the life of God himself. Your earthly parents gave life from their living bodies which became your life when you were born. In the same way God, in imparting to you his own life, became your heavenly Father. You are a child of God in a *literal* sense.

But the life must grow and develop. As it does, you will reflect, more and more, the likeness of the Father from whom the life came. As God's life within you grows, it will influence both your emotional and your physical development. You will become more mature emotionally. Other things being equal, you will enjoy better physical health. Your new birth does not guarantee that you will never be emotionally or physically sick, but it will move you in the direction of improved health.

For your new life to grow, it must be fed and exercised. The food it requires is the holy Scriptures. Exercise will consist of obedience by faith to the commands of God. You will also need to breathe deep drafts of heavenly air as your prayer life develops. All of these factors that contribute to your spiritual growth will be examined carefully in the chapters that follow. For the present it is enough to know that you are a hybrid—a being with two types of life and two sets of parentage.

NEW RELATIONSHIPS WITH GOD AND PEOPLE

The events that have occurred to you include dramatic changes in your personal relationships. Once alienated from God, you have changed to being at peace with him as well as being his child. Christ, his unique Son whom you may formerly have ignored, now has a relationship with you, and you with him, which is many-faceted. He is your Shepherd, and you are his sheep. As time goes on you will become increasingly expert at discerning his voice and being able to follow wherever he leads. And he guarantees you refreshment and rest, provided you follow him, and a determination to bring you back to the flock should you stray and get lost.

He is also your Master, and you his slave. He always had the right to treat you as a slave, but he never whipped you into submission. Implicit in your new relationship is a recognition on your part that you *are* his slave and will allow him the right to govern your entire life. For though he demands obedience, you have the power to deny him his rights. In doing so you would dishonor him and damage your spiritual well-being. Nevertheless, he refuses to turn you into an automaton or to be brutal to you.

He is also your "great high priest." At those times when feelings of weakness and frustration crush you, you will find fresh courage when you remember your high priest is still human as well as divine. Having personally experienced every human temptation and stress, he can understand how you feel. He sympathizes with your weakness. Because of his eternal humanness, he is uniquely equipped both to support you and to plead for you.

We could discuss many facets of your relationship with Christ. He is your captain in battle and you his soldier. He is the bread on whom you feed. He is the light illuminating your interior darkness. And so we could go on. What in essence all of this means is that you now belong to him and he to you in a relationship of vital interchanges. Bonds have been established between you that nothing in heaven, earth or hell can break.

Many of your other relationships have changed too. For instance, you are now part of an innumerable company of redeemed human beings, both here and beyond death. You are a co-citizen with martyrs and apostles. Though my words may conjure up in your mind visions of swords, robes and sandals, your heavenly citizenship also has to do with mundane relationships in everyday life.

If you were brought up in a large family, you may have noticed that it was more difficult to get on with your brothers and sisters than with friends outside the family. But at times of crisis, you would all unite. But at other times tensions would exist. Do not be surprised then to discover tensions within your heavenly family. Your brothers and sisters in Christ are not perfect. After the first happy glow, during which you may idealize them, you will be shocked to discover bitterness, bickering and overt hostility in the Christian family.

You will also discover that some Christians are stupid, ornery, tactless; "stuffed shirts," prudes, hypocrites and so on.

Some will be bigoted advocates of totally unacceptable political positions, and others will slurp their soup or have bad breath. We shall come to the complex question of how you relate to them later on. For the present it is enough that you remember that God loves them even though you find it hard to. You must also be charitable enough to admit that there may be unattractive features in your own personality.

Finally, you must realize that the same new life that is in you is in them. Look well at their faults and see for yourself that the miracle of new life does not guarantee beauty of character. The life needs to grow and develop. That is why I am writing this book. I feel a great urge inside me to share with you as much as I can of what is important in practical Christian living.

A FOE OF LEGIONS

You have also established a new relationship with the powers of darkness. Whatever you were before you became a Christian— straight, horoscope reader, witch, warlock or Satanist—you are now the sworn foe of the legions of hell.

Have no delusions about their reality or their hostility. But do not fear them. The God inside you terrifies them. They cannot touch you, let alone hurt you. But they can still seduce and they will try. They will also oppose you as you obey Christ. If you play it cool and decide not to be a fanatic about Christianity, you will have no trouble from them. But if you are serious about Christ being your Lord and God, you can expect opposition.

"Resist the devil," writes James, "and he will flee from you" (Jas 4:7). Life with Jesus can be an exhilarating and reassuring experience of constant triumph over evil forces. But the battle never ends.

What both of us must realize is that you have been given a personal tutor. His coming to you is the most important event associated with your becoming a Christian. Whether you felt his coming or not, the Holy Spirit has taken up his dwelling place in you. Christ's object in sending him was to insure that you get even better instruction than the apostles had by having Jesus in their midst. You may lament the fact that Jesus is no longer here physically. But as Jesus sees it, you have a greater privilege by having God's Spirit inside you.

The Holy Spirit is a self-effacing person. He does not wish to tell you much about himself, preferring rather to instruct you about Christ and your relationship with him. You can learn about the Holy Spirit by reading certain passages in John's Gospel, which are listed at the end of this chapter. It is the Holy Spirit who will make truth come alive for you by enabling you to grasp it clearly, by reminding you of things he has previously taught you, by drilling you in difficult exercises that get at your personality weaknesses, by encouraging you when you are down, by echoing the good Shepherd's voice in your hearing and in many other ways. If you rely on *him* rather than on mechanical devices or religious exercises (both of which have a place) you will grow.

You may have periods of darkness or of doubt. You may encounter painful struggles and discouragement. But there will also be moments of exultation and glory. And most important of all, you will become free.

A PASSAGE TO STUDY

Don't read chapter two yet. Instead, spend half an hour quietly praying over the following passages. Make notes on them and try to answer the questions. Choose a modern translation if you have one.

Read John 14:15-26—these verses form part of Christ's final briefing session with the apostles.

1. Compare verse 16 (in which "another Counselor" would come to the apostles and stay with them forever) with verses 18 and 20. We are told that the Holy Spirit, a person in his own right, is also the Spirit of Jesus and the Father. This is hard for us to grasp. What support would such an idea find in this passage?

2. What functions of the Holy Spirit are described here? Make a note of them and remember that the same Holy Spirit dwells in your body too.

3. Read John 15:26—16:15. What further functions of the Holy Spirit are described? How would they apply in your own life?

4. I have suggested that the Holy Spirit is self-effacing. What support does John's Gospel lend to this idea?

2

Prayer

When I was a medical student in England, someone in the Inter-Varsity group gave me a card that changed my life. On it were a couple of quotations from the Gospels indicating how Jesus once spent all night in prayer. Underneath the texts was one brief sentence ending, "God helping me I resolve to spend at least twenty minutes daily in prayer to God." Below this was a dotted line where I signed my name.

The powerful appeal the card made to me must have had some explanation. It could have been its simplicity. The color and lettering certainly appealed to me aesthetically. Obviously there was more to it than either of these things, however. Thirty years have passed. Today a quiet song of joy is still flowing from my heart because of the ongoing revolution that little card began.

There are a number of ways of looking at it. I must have had some inner longing to which the card appealed. Again, the need must have been met, since my changed behavior has lasted long past my initial resolve.

DEEP CALLS TO DEEP

For the last ten years I have been watching the Manitoba spring. As snow melts, water trickles, then hurries into pools, lakes, floods. In front of our house a little lake stretches across the roadway to the delight of the small children and the annoyance of their seniors. There are drain openings on both sides of the street in the curbs of the sidewalks. The water is deepest by the drain openings. It affords me vast satisfaction every spring to plunge my hands into the cold water, seize the accumulation of dead leaves and twigs blocking the drain and then watch the eager rush of water into its thirsty jaws.

My little card produced a release of that kind in my life. It unplugged me. I was set free.

I mention the fact because usually sermons on prayer stress either its importance or our Christian duty to pray. Indeed the implication of the words on my card was that if Jesus prayed, I ought to do so too. If he, the God-man, needed close contact with the Father in prayer, how much more did I?

Well it is our duty to pray, and it is an important duty. The Scriptures themselves emphasize this. "Pray constantly" (1 Thess 5:17). "In everything by prayer and supplication with thanksgiving let your requests be made known to God" (Phil 4:6). "Pray at all times in the Spirit, with all prayer and supplication. To that end keep alert with all perseverance" (Eph 6:18). We "ought always to pray and not lose heart" (Lk 18:1).

But if all we knew was that it was *our duty* to pray or how important it was to pray, we would be in sorry straits. You can be earnest and duty bound only so long—and after that the effort becomes intolerable. My card did not only stir my conscience into action. It awoke hope in me. I felt no pride as I signed it, only joy and a sense of expectation.

Years earlier I had attempted to pray. Dissatisfied with the quality of my Christian life and having read some (now forgotten) exhortation on prayer, I set my alarm for 6 a.m., determined to begin the day with two hours of prayer and Bible study. It was winter. English houses are not only dark but miserably cold in the early morning. My eyes were sore. My nose ran and I shivered. The silent house seemed strangely unfriendly. Determinedly I prayed—for my immediate family; for distant cousins, uncles, aunts; for neighbors and friends. Then I looked at my watch to find that only five minutes had gone by. Somehow I had to carry on for another hour and fifty-five minutes. Time stretched ahead like a cold eternity.

I managed to keep on praying for twenty-five minutes, by which time I had exhausted every possible topic of prayer. A little uncertain of myself I decided that it might be appropriate to study the Bible. Not knowing where to start, I elected to master Paul's epistle to the Romans. I read with a vague sense of dissatisfaction. How did one study the Bible? I frowned and tried to concentrate, but the words stared back at me inscrutably, coldly determined to hold their own counsel.

Somehow I managed to go on frowning and reading for the rest of the two hours. But I was licked, and I knew it. I kept going for another two days, but on the third day I acknowledged my defeat and crawled miserably back to bed thirty-five minutes after I got up.

After that I put prayer and Bible study out of my mind. It was for saints and martyrs. I was not made of praying stuff. But I felt guilty, depressed and cheated.

Somewhere within me I had been hoping, even longing, for

I knew not what. I had thought that by going through my performance of sacrificial prayer my longing would be satisfied. If satisfaction did not come to me, then my faith (or my capacity for sacrifice) was inadequate. The riches I craved were there. I yearned for them. But I was capable only of so much. So I stifled my longings.

But where had those longings come from? Did they represent an accumulation of frustrations for which I sought a magical and unrealistic answer? Was I being flung back to face "reality" and told to solve my problems in ways other than prayer fantasies? Or was the longing divinely planted?

In the first chapter of Augustine's book *Confessions* are his oft-quoted words "for Thou hast made us for Thyself; and our hearts are restless, till they find their rest in Thee." Augustine's answer is the correct one. Frustrations we may have, but they are beside the point. We were designed for fellowship with God, and without that fellowship we ache in emptiness. He himself planted the longing there, a longing all of us share. And God plays his sweet music causing the longing to throb and come to life.

Deep within your vast interior spaces (and inner space and outer space are all one in eternity) is a tabernacle God built to commune with you. From it he calls you with tender urgency. And from the furthest reaches of your inner space an ache of yearning echoes back his call.

You may ignore it. At times you do so because the excitement of other attractions appeals to you more. But they appeal to the surface of your being. They create anxiety, whereas his call is a call to peace.

Or perhaps you fear that you are unworthy to approach the

tabernacle, much less to enter it. There seem so many apologies that you ought to make to God, so many problems, so much insincerity to overcome before you could begin to get close. And so you are alienated, living not only far from the God within you but far from the depths of your own being. You live on the surface of your life while Deep is calling to deep.

GOD IN SEARCH OF MAN

The first thing you must learn about prayer is that God wants fellowship with you and is drawing you to himself. To change the metaphor: He is pursuing you. He is waiting to trap you into an encounter with himself. He does so not because he needs you but because you need him. His is the tenderness of a mother over a fretful infant. Prayer is to turn inwardly (or outwardly— it is all one), enter the tabernacle where he waits and let him speak with you. For he is there. And he is speaking. And you may sit in quietness to drink in his beauty, trembling with joy.

But it may take time to learn the confidence of going into the presence of the One who calls you. Many books on prayer stress techniques for doing so. I believe only two things are necessary. First, you must recognize the Holy Spirit has already become your teacher. Don't ask how *you* can best cooperate with him. The teaching and training is *his* job, and in his own way and time he will teach you.

Second, you must let the truth of what I am saying sink into your heart in quietness. Remind yourself constantly of the words of Scripture: "Draw near to God and he will draw near to you" (Jas 4:8). Memorize such verses of the Bible as:

Therefore, brethren, since we have confidence to enter

the sanctuary by the blood of Jesus, by the new and living way which he opened for us, . . . and since we have a great priest over the house of God, let us draw near with a true heart in full assurance of faith, with our hearts sprinkled clean from an evil conscience. (Heb 10:19-22)

Up to now, I have been trying to get two things across to you. First, the initiative in prayer lies with God. Second, you were designed to respond to his initiative. Your business and your deepest satisfaction will be to respond to the overtures that he is making.

But I would expose you to two dangers were I to leave the matter there. First, I might leave you with the impression that all you need to do is to wait silently and try to listen to God's voice. The other danger is that you might confuse prayer with something like Transcendental Meditation. For certainly what I have written opens the door to possibilities of unearthly rapture.

There is a fundamental difference between meditative techniques and prayer. The object of such techniques is to achieve an altered state of consciousness—a relaxed, detached mental state sought for the well being that may result from the exercise.

When a Christian prays, he or she is not aiming at an altered state of consciousness. Nor when God calls us to pray does he offer us a trip. His aim is that we may have fellowship with him, a person who really exists. Whether altered states of consciousness or feelings accompany prayer is neither here nor there. Usually they don't, except in some minor degree. Occasionally, like Paul, we may be caught up "into Paradise . . . and [hear] things that cannot be told, which man may not utter" (2 Cor 12:2-4).

Ecstasy may come rarely and to a few, but it is never to be sought. It is no mark of special favor. What must be sought is fellowship with a real person. And this brings me to the first problem I raised.

As I wait in silence, I am not opening my being to a Mysterious Unknown. I am listening for the God of the Scriptures, the God whose tabernacle has been built in my innermost being. And as I penetrate that sanctuary I will encounter the God whom Jesus revealed and whom the Scriptures describe. It is to the One who has revealed himself already that I must come.

An unknown English mystic of the twelfth century wrote a profoundly influential book known as *The Cloud of the Unknowing*. I meditated long and prayerfully on *The Cloud*, and as I did so I saw clearly where true Christianity and some forms of mysticism part company. The author of *The Cloud* exhorts us to put all that we know about God under the dark cloud of unknowing, stripping ourselves of every idea or concept of God, confessing that we cannot know, except as we penetrate into the blackness with "the pure intent of naked love."

Sounds great. It has "blown the minds" of people of profound devotion and brilliant intellect for the past eight hundred years. And it is true that we cannot understand the God we approach in prayer. His thoughts are not our thoughts. His ways surpass our capacity to grasp. Because he transcends all we can understand or know, we speak of the *transcendence* of God. But we are not invited to know what cannot be known until a coming day. And if God has gone to such pains, through the prophets and by means of the incarnation, to reveal to us what we can understand of him, is it not irreverent folly and vanity to cast aside all that he has revealed at such cost for the vain benefit of a supposed "higher" experience? All we may be achieving is some altered states of consciousness.

The God of the universe has made himself comprehensible to our finite minds. The God of the Scriptures seeks fellowship with us. He will always remain mysterious, but it will be the mystery of our dearly loved, truly known Father. (What child *understands* the earthly father he knows so intimately?)

Therefore, be simple and practical in your approach to God. Have a look at your daily schedule and see where and how you can arrange for twenty minutes of unhurried, quiet waiting on God every day. Choose a place where you are unlikely to be distracted, and go there regularly.

There is nothing magical about a time span of twenty minutes. It is a starting point that most inexperienced pray-ers find helpful. You need about that length of time so as to be unrushed, unhurried. If you later find you need more time, no problem.

Begin by remembering that he seeks you and longs to speak with you. If you feel fuddleheaded first thing in the morning, wash and dress before your quiet time. Should you still feel flat as lukewarm Coke, don't worry. Simply begin by thanking God that whether you feel him or not, you know he has been waiting for you. Then instruct your soul repeatedly as the psalmist did: "For God alone my soul waits in silence, for my hope is from him" (Ps 62:5).

How you proceed from there will depend on what you discover, under the Spirit's gentle guidance, to be helpful.

The Spirit will teach you *worship*, which means expressing to God how worthy he is. He will also teach you *praise* and *thanksgiving*. Some of the psalms may be helpful here. There is nothing wrong with reading one of them aloud as an act of worship to God. Some of them (such as Ps 30:1-3) may express your feelings better than your own words can. You may even find that some of the great prayers of the past (like those of Lancelot Andrewes) are helpful. Or you may be freer expressing praise and worship in your own words.

Confession of sin is not only helpful but essential if your relationship to God is to remain clear. Talking over problems, *supplications* (asking for things you want), *intercessions* (asking things for other people) are all part of prayer. The thing to remember is that God is intensely interested in the smallest details of your own and other people's lives. To realize this does not make one's prayers self-centered, but paradoxically it is a way to avoid the danger of self-centeredness.

Are there things about God or the Bible that trouble you? Are you upset over the injustices and hypocrisies of those around you? God cares. He wants you to share these things with him. As you do so you will begin to marvel at an infinite God who is concerned with your petty problems and who does not dismiss them as petty. Because they are important to you, they are to him too.

As for your personal requests, he has already anticipated them. He is waiting for you to make them. You do not have to twist his arm. I personally wait eagerly for my children to come to me to ask me for their allowances or to request me to read a story. When they fail to ask, I am disappointed. God has, unknown to you, been encouraging you to make some requests before you ever began to formulate them in your mind. And as for other requests that would be wrong for him to grant to you, he is only too happy that you have the confidence to be frank about them.

For prayer is not *you* trying to move *God*. Prayer is *being caught up* into God's directions and activity. He orders the affairs of the universe and invites you to participate by prayer. Intercession is God and you in partnership, bringing his perfect plans into being.

PRAYER LANGUAGE

What words ought you to use in prayer? Do you say "Thee" and "Thou" or "You" when addressing God? Should you always end prayer with the words, "In the name of the Lord Jesus Christ. Amen"?

There are no rules. God is not concerned with the form of your words but with the honesty and reverence of your heart. The more he teaches you about himself and the more aware you become of him, the more your words and attitude will be appropriate. Let God make you aware of himself, then be yourself in the presence of the holy One.

As for using the words, "in the name of Jesus," everything depends on why you use them. If they are used superstitiously (as a kind of spell that magically gives your prayer some extra zing), they had better be dropped.

Why are they used at all?

They should make you aware of two things. In using them you are reminding yourself of the grounds for your right to enter God's presence. You would have no right to approach God the Father if it were not through the redeeming work of God the Son. It is wise to use the words, from time to time at least, so that you remember this.

The words are also used when making requests. Jesus himself made it clear that requests "in my name" would never be refused by the Father (Jn 14:13-14). A request made "in the name of Jesus," means a request that he authorizes. Jesus gave his followers authority to draw checks on the power bank of heaven. Clearly, however, the checks may only be drawn when the purpose of the check conforms with heavenly policy. It is only when I am acting as Christ's agent that I may pray "in his name."

I am the president of a certain provincial association. Along with the treasurer I have authority to sign checks *in the name of* the association. The bank will honor my checks when they are so drawn up and signed by me. It would even be possible for me to cash association checks for my personal pleasures. Possible— but wrong.

In the case of heaven's bank, prayers that terminate with the words "in the name of Jesus" but do not reflect the will of Jesus will not be honored. Heaven can spot what an earthly teller cannot.

Rightly understood, then, the expression "in the name of Jesus" can be an effective guard against praying drivel. Remember that prayer consists of collaborating with God in his divine purposes. If the words we are discussing remind you of this and cause you to weigh your requests carefully before making them, they serve a valuable purpose.

Have I any right to ask the Father to help me get an A on my term paper "in the name of Jesus"? It depends what my term paper has to do with his purposes. The apparent triviality of my request has no bearing on the problem. The fact that my term paper will mean nothing twenty years from now is irrelevant. To dry a single tear can be entirely within God's eternal purposes. What matters is whether my request conforms to his will.

But how can I know this? We will talk later about knowing

God's will in the chapter on guidance. For the present the following principles will help:

1. It is always God's will that we praise him, thank him and confess our sins.

2. It is always God's will that we be open with him about the longings of our heart. It is perfectly legitimate to tell him "Lord, I'd really like to get an A on my paper. It means a lot to me." He likes us to share with him (Ps 103:13) even though he may not always give us what we want.

3. It is always God's will that we pray for our enemies (Mt 5:44).

4. The more we learn about the Bible, the more we understand what God's view of things is. The more we understand about his outlook, the more we know what his will is in a given instance.

5. There are specific promises in the Bible. It is always God's will that when we pray, we take these promises seriously and count on their fulfillment.

6. When we are puzzled about what God's will *might* be, we are encouraged to ask for wisdom. We should do so with complete confidence that we will be given the understanding we need (Jas 1:5-7).

The word *amen* is used too often as a habit. In conventional prayer it tells you when the prayer has ended. Through long custom it has become a verbalized period. In the Bible *amen* has various meanings and could be translated "truth," "truly" or "so be it" according to the context. When Jesus used to say "verily, verily," the Greek term employed is a transliteration of the Hebrew word *amen*.

The most dramatic amens are found in the book of Revelation, usually following a chorus of praise to God and the Lamb. In those instances the beings surrounding the throne express their hearty approval of the praises by using *amen* to mean something like, "Yes, O Lord, that is absolutely right!"

Perhaps this is the most appropriate way to use the word today. You will find that in the less inhibited prayer meetings, people will signify their agreement with what someone else is praying by saying, "Amen, Lord! Amen!" Others will say, "Yes, Lord! Yes!" Since God is fluent in Hebrew and English, he probably doesn't mind which language is used and is glad that his children are united in their prayers.

Should we drop the amen at the end of prayers? If it is used to mean "end of paragraph" or "prayer now over," the answer is yes. But there are occasions when it is appropriate. For instance, to request something "in the name of Jesus. Amen!" means *"let this be so* in this name of Jesus." Of course we might just as well say it in English as in Hebrew.

There is no magic in the Hebrew tongue. The point is that using the words "let this be so" reminds the person praying of the solemnity and the definiteness of the petition he or she is making. It says, "I am not just talking into thin air. This is a real request. Let it become reality."

Another occasion when it might be appropriate is when you make a positive affirmation of praise in prayer. At the end of the Lord's Prayer, for instance, are the words "For Thine is the kingdom, the power, and the glory, for ever and ever. *And that's absolutely true, and I affirm it.*" (For that is what *amen* means in that context.)

Whether you say your amens in English or in Hebrew is entirely up to you. So long as your inner eyes are turned upon the

God of heaven, the language you employ will be relatively unimportant. But when praying with others, sometimes there is value in conforming to their customs, provided you do not feel too unnatural in doing so.

PRAYING IN PUBLIC

You will probably find it deeply rewarding to join other Christians in prayer. In our society when Christians meet for prayer, they usually pray one at a time. In this way everyone can participate in everyone else's prayer.

You may find yourself inhibited at first. Some Christians display verbal expertise in prayer. Some can use *Thee* and *Thou* fluently and with the correct verbs. Others are experts in "conversational prayer," and you may be unsure when they're through—because they don't say amen. Any form of prayer (conversational or conventional) can be an exercise in eloquence, a piece of subtle showmanship or a sincere prayer. It can also be intimidating to the uninitiated.

Try praying with one Christian friend to start off. Then when you go to a larger prayer session, concentrate your thoughts on the God to whom you are all praying and not on the people who pray. It matters little what others think of your prayer. God wants to hear it. And *he* wants others to share it. If you can keep God in the center of your thoughts, you will be less likely to view public prayer as a performance.

Don't worry about your voice sounding shaky or squeaky. Just go ahead and talk to God. He will be delighted to hear your words, and new links of fellowship will be forged with the other Christians around you. Some of them will be encouraged to pray because you prayed. Others will be glad about the subject of your prayer and echo it fervently in their hearts.

HEARING GOD'S VOICE

So far I have been evading the issue of how you hear God speaking when you pray. Jesus said, "My sheep hear my voice, . . . and they follow me" (Jn 10:27). How do you distinguish between your own thoughts or wishes and the voice of the Shepherd? Isn't it very easy to fool yourself? Worse still, isn't it possible to mistake evil voices for the voice of the Shepherd?

Let me get back to my basic point. It is God who wishes to establish communication. He is more anxious to speak to us than we are to hear him. He is incredibly persistent in trying to get through. Our real problem is that we tend to *avoid* hearing him.

Difficulties arise. First, let me say that when Jesus said, "My sheep hear my voice," he was saying something a little different from what we commonly read into the verse. Our first impression is that he is telling us that from somewhere within us promptings will come, promptings accompanied by an infallible knowledge that Jesus is their origin. That is not exactly what he was saying.

To hear, in the Bible, usually carries the connotation of to *pay heed to*. Thus a follower of Jesus is someone who takes God's injunctions seriously. A follower is distinguished from other "sheep" by the fact that he or she is determined to follow only the true Shepherd. When other voices clamor for attention, a follower deliberately closes his or her ears to them. Only one voice will be obeyed.

And because a follower is determined to obey one voice alone, he or she will learn to distinguish that voice from others (Jn 7:17). It may take time to do so. After all, lambs do not at first distinguish the Shepherd's voice, only the voice of the ewe.

In practical terms this means that as a Christian matures and increases in the understanding of divine things, he or she will become increasingly able to spot truth and distinguish it from error. It also means that the capacity to do so will be proportionate to his or her determination to obey the Lord.

But doesn't God also speak directly so that we have precise guidance with precise problems? Of course he does. However God's main concern is to communicate *moral* guidance to us and to speak to us about right, wrong and how to relate to himself. And it is in this area that we should consider the use of the Bible in prayer.

THE BIBLE AND PRAYER

Experienced pray-ers like to have a Bible handy when they pray. Some commence prayer with a reading from a daily devotional. Others read Scripture systematically.

Since I will discuss Bible study more fully in chapter three, I will limit myself here to dealing with negative points. There are dangers in using the Bible (or reading guides). Many Christians I know look on their Bibles as horoscopes. They approach them armed with specific worries and hope that God will "speak" to them from their daily reading of Scripture.

The tragedy of this approach is that when you adopt it, you tend to miss the real teaching of a passage, screening it out through the filter of your own hopes and fears. You distort and twist the passage to make it fit like a poultice over your spiritual boils.

God sometimes will take a passage and with peculiar directness speak to you about a problem in your life. Remember, he is the One who wishes to communicate and who can use many ways of doing so. But for you to come to his Word insisting that it *say what you want it to say* is to close your ears to what God may really be telling you.

If you have a problem, by all means unburden yourself before God. Leave the matter confidently with him. And as you turn to the Scriptures, put your problem out of your mind and seek what God is really saying in the passage.

DAYDREAMING

From time to time you will find your thoughts straying far away from God and prayer. This can be disconcerting and discouraging. When my thoughts wandered, I used to say, "Oh, I'm sorry, Lord, I wish I didn't wander like this. Please help me not to . . ." and then off I would go into another daydream.

The causes of daydreams are many, tiredness being the most common. I know no way of avoiding them, but it is important to react rightly when you realize what you are doing.

What is it, do you think, that brings you back to the point? Or better still, who is it? When I discover myself daydreaming, my response now is, "Thank you, Lord. Thank you for rescuing me again. I would waste a lot more time daydreaming if it weren't for you." I don't grovel. I don't waste time in bitter self-recrimination or in discouragement. I rejoice in the infinite patience of God, who never gives up and who calls me constantly back to himself.

THE PRACTICE OF THE PRESENCE

It is good to have a set time to meet with God daily. But it becomes a bad thing if you feel that communion is confined to that brief period. Meister Eckhart, an old mystic, urged Christians to carry from their secret meeting with God "the same frame of mind" into the world around them. You see, you do not leave God when you go from the quiet place any more than he leaves you. A quiet time is a "tuning in" time. You should not switch off the radio once you have tuned in to God's wavelength. In *Testament of Devotion* Thomas Kelly talks about living on two planes at once. Impossible as it may seem, it is the unusual privilege of the Christian to be aware of God at all times. In *The Practice of the Presence of God* Brother Lawrence speaks simply and straight-forwardly of the same thing.

You need not constantly be formulating verbal petitions, but like the psalmist you may enjoy the Lord "always before your face." It may be that such a practice is what Paul refers to when he urges us to "Pray constantly" (1 Thess 5:17). You may leave the room where you pray, but you do not have to leave the inner sanctuary deep inside your being.

Still, old habits of mind may be hard to overcome. Most of the time, whether we are aware of it or not, our minds are occupied at the same time with the intellectual tasks on hand or how much time we have or a hundred other things. Pure concentration on one task is almost impossible. Our minds function simultaneously on various levels, even when we are concentrating hard on a mathematical problem. The capacity to carry out our tasks efficiently while we continue to praise God presents no difficulty as far as our brain function is concerned. Our difficulty is simply that old habits of thought want to reassert themselves and crowd out what is most needed.

The Holy Spirit wishes to make us more aware of God at all times. Just as we wander in thought when having devotions, we will constantly wander in thought all day long. And each time we become aware of doing so, it is because God is getting through to us again. Don't waste time kicking yourself when you wake up to the fact that your thoughts have been anywhere but where they should be. Immediately say, "Thank you, Lord. Thank you because you never cease to speak to me. Thank you that you are always near."

SUMMARY

We have learned that God constantly seeks communion with us. Prayer consists of responding to God. We should set aside a period every day specifically for prayer. During that time we should give ourselves to worship and thanksgiving, to confession, to fellowship and to petitions and intercession. No special form is needed, but the Spirit will teach us reverence as we wait on God. As we leave our formal quiet time, we should let God teach us the secret of remaining in his presence throughout the day.

A FEW SUGGESTIONS

1. Passages to use in praise and worship. (Try singing them to music you make up as you go along.)
   Psalm 92:1-5
   Psalm 93:1-5
   Psalm 95:1-11
   Psalm 96:1-13
   Psalm 97:1-12
   Psalm 100:1-5
   Psalm 103:1-22

2. Books to read.

Prayer, by Ole Hallesby.
The Practice of the Presence of God, by Brother Lawrence.
A Testament of Devotion, by Thomas Kelly.

3. A commitment to consider.

- "And in the morning, a great while before day, he rose and went out to a lonely place, and there he prayed." (Mk 1:35)
- "In these days he went out to the mountains to pray; and all night he continued in prayer to God." (Lk 6:12)
- I resolve, by the help of God, to set aside at least twenty minutes every day to spend alone in God's presence.

Signed

Date

3

God Still Speaks

———— 🌿 ————

They seemed an unlikely bunch. I was sure they were bona fide Christians. I had led them to Christ myself. Yet just as I would be feeling reassured that they were turning out well, they would do and say the strangest things. I clucked over them like a nervous hen, worried lest I had hatched swans.

We were all students in the same residence hall. Somehow they did not conform to my stereotype of a Christian. Not that conforming to a stereotype was important, but they just didn't seem to be "tuned in."

Yet one year later I had no hesitation in calling them godly. They knew what they believed and knew where they were going in life. They had become Christians. The only way I can account for the difference was that during the intervening months we all had been studying Scripture steadily, both individually and collectively.

Pat, a six-foot, genial athlete, was another guy who had me

worried. Friendly, helpful, but clueless. On impulse I loaned him a book about daily Bible study and didn't see him again for six months. When we ran across each other later, I was astounded. Same face. Same build. Different man.

I had forgotten about the book, but Pat hadn't. "It changed my life," he told me seriously, "at least, daily, prayerful Bible study did." It was not the sort of language he would have used six months before.

Pat has now been a missionary for many years. I need not have been surprised. Scripture claims to have profound effects on us. "Like newborn babes," writes Peter, "desire the sincere milk of the word, *that ye may grow thereby*" (1 Pet 2:2 KJV).

In chapter one I pointed out that the very life of God was planted within you when you became a Christian. You were born again. I also pointed out that spiritual life, like biological life, has its own developmental needs, one of which is truth. As you absorb truth from Scripture, spiritual life will thrive within you. As Peter says, you will grow as you feed on the milk of the Word.

Scripture truth is more than milk, however. It varies in texture and substance, and correspondingly in ease of digestion. The more you develop spiritually the better able you will be to stomach the meat of Scripture. Strong truth makes strong Christians stronger.

Scripture also gives you clear moral guidelines to live by. They will not always be in the form of simple do's and don'ts. God designed Scripture to give moral orientation to people living in any culture, in any age and in any moral climate.

Your sense of right and wrong was developed by your upbringing and by other moral influences surrounding you. If you were reared by parents who were strong-minded teetotalers, you will feel uneasy if you start to drink irrespective of the real morality of drinking. People in some savage tribes kill under certain circumstances with a feeling of doing a virtuous thing. Few people in North America would feel the same way. You may even have questioned whether absolute rights and wrongs exist.

They do. God himself is the absolute standard, and while such matters as motive and local custom are of great importance, there are moral absolutes in the very structure of the universe. But how do you find them? How can consciences be reoriented?

Scripture sheds light on morality because it reveals God himself. Study it with a willingness to pay the cost of obedience, and order will gradually replace confusion. "How can a young man keep his way pure? By guarding it according to thy word" (Ps 119:9).

But Scripture will do more. Truth liberates. It not only reveals a standard but will set you free to keep it. This is what makes Scripture so different from other ethical systems, which are powerless to help the struggler. You may not experience Scripture's full effect at once, but as time goes on, it will become increasingly influential in shaping your behavior. "I have laid up thy word in my heart, that I might not sin against thee" (Ps 119:11).

The change will not be without conflict. There is a personal devil. Habit will be on his side as he actively opposes your attempts to live as God would have you live. Notice that the weapon most effective in countering his attacks according to Paul is "the sword of the Spirit, which is the word of God" (Eph 6:17). A knowledge of Scripture is invaluable when you encounter the power of darkness.

There are other things Scripture will do for you. It will make you wise: wiser than people around you, wiser than your professors. Notice, I said *wiser*, not more knowledgeable. A wise person is one who can distinguish what is fundamental from what is trivial, who knows what life is about and who acts appropriately whatever the circumstances.

In the university there are many people who can impress us with incomprehensible twaddle. There are also brilliant people. But few are wise. "I have more understanding than all my teachers," wrote a psalmist long ago, "for thy testimonies are my meditation. I understand more than the aged, for I keep thy precepts" (Ps 119:99-100).

Wisdom, you must understand, is always humble and open to learn. The wisdom that God gives through Scripture does not lead you to quote a Bible verse to contradict a biology professor's assertions. Such actions spring from bigotry and naiveté rather than godly wisdom.

Later on I speak of guidance in a Christian's life and about what part Scripture plays in it. The same psalmist I have already quoted wrote, "Thy word is a lamp to my feet and a light to my path." (Ps 119:105). However, he was talking about *a moral* pathway rather than a geographic one. The Bible is not a horoscope. Never try to read into Scripture mysterious instructions about your daily activities.

Neither is the Bible a sedative. It does not tranquilize. Yet in reading it you will find peace. "Great peace have those who love thy law" (Ps 119:165). Chemical tranquilizing agents can work by blunting the impact reality has on you. Scripture imparts peace by showing you how to resolve any inner conflicts that destroy peace.

Peace is more than the absence of anxiety. It is a positive quality arising from inner harmony. A peace that is destroyed by external threats is no peace. God's peace, which will grow the more you understand Scripture, defies uncertainty and danger. It is the clear-eyed peace with which the Roman Christians faced hungry lions in ancient arenas and with which many Christians today face imprisonment, torture and threats to their families. It is a peace which comes from the understanding that God is in charge, that you belong to him and that chaos and uncertainty around you represent only the confusing surface of reality.

And such peace, understandably, improves your physical well being. It is "marrow to your bones."

PRACTICAL PROBLEMS

I could continue to list the benefits of regular Scripture reading, but why should I? The living God has spoken. The ruler of the universe has revealed himself in print. Yet still we hesitate. Why?

You may, of course, have doubts that the Bible is inspired by God. You may feel uncomfortable precisely because you are supposed to approach it with reverence or with a special set of feelings, which you cannot produce because of your inner doubts.

The best way to deal with those inner doubts is to expose yourself to the Bible. Don't approach it with any special feelings, except for a willingness to put into practice any truth you see in it. I could argue about inspiration, but I refuse to. Find out for yourself. The least we can say about the Bible is that it is a compilation of historical documents whose validity (as historical data) is now above reproach. Read it and let it speak to you.

Pray, "Please show me, O God, if these documents *do* constitute your Word." But read openly. Try to understand what is actually being said. Be willing to incorporate whatever truth you see into your own life.

"Ah, you have me there," a research scientist once confessed to me thoughtfully. "I'm not sure I can take the risk. It might mean leaving my job and being a missionary or something." He was not joking. Few people are quite so honest, and I could offer him no guarantees as to what demands might be made of him.

On the other hand your problem may be the very opposite. You may be *too* conscious of the Bible's unique character—so conscious, in fact, that you are inhibited when you read.

Many years ago in Latin America I was astonished to discover that Roman Catholic students (who in those days had had little or no exposure to Scripture) and communist students were far better at Bible study than students from evangelical churches. In group study the communists and Catholics were quick to see what the passage *actually said.* Many evangelical students, on the other hand, had a mental block at this point. They seemed only able to see what the Bible *was supposed to say.* It was as though they screened Bible statements through a doctrinal filter, seeing only what they had been trained to expect. ("It can't say *that* because the Bible doesn't teach that.")

Or maybe you expect some kind of magic. I think that was my problem years ago in my chilly early morning experiments. I had a preconceived notion as to *how* God would speak from Scripture. When what I expected did not take place, I was confused and disappointed.

Scripture is not magic. It is truth expressed in words, sentences and paragraphs. (The verse numbers and chapter headings were imposed by translators long after the original documents were compiled.) But someone will object, "Isn't it true that the Bible can only be understood when the Holy Spirit opens our understanding and speaks to us from it?" Quite so. But the question almost implies that the Holy Spirit needs to be persuaded. It seems to suggest that before he can speak, you have to go through a special "tuning in" session or that the words themselves are difficult and obscure, so that only if you are in some specially inspired condition can obscurity be resolved into profundity.

God's desire is to make matters plain to anyone, anytime, anywhere. In addition to providing us with documents that are for the most part simply and clearly written, he quickens our minds by his Spirit, provided we genuinely want to know. Pride, prejudice and preconceptions are the big barriers to seeing truth. Be humble. Look at what is there. Tell God you know your mind has limitations. Thank him that he will help you understand.

Of course we use the word *understand* in two ways. Sometimes when we say, "I don't understand," we mean, "I can't grasp what the writer is trying to say." At other times we mean, "I can see what he's saying all right, but I don't see how it could be true."

Both types of problem can arise when you read Scripture. The problem of the words not making sense often resolves itself when you use a modern translation. The second kind of problem ("I see what it says, but I can't believe it's true") is a sign that you are thinking about what you are reading. People who never hit problems of this sort are only going through the motions of reading.

The first thing to do is to make sure you *have* read the passage correctly. You may be puzzling over something it didn't say in the first place. But if having checked, you are still shaking your head, there are many steps you can take.

You are not likely to be the first person to be puzzled. Chances are that many people have already wrestled with the same problem. Some of their thoughts will be recorded in Bible commentaries. You may be puzzled simply because the Scripture conflicts with your prior ideas about what the Bible *ought* to say. But in any case, remember that in learning about the most profound mysteries of being, you are likely to come across ideas that shake and disturb you. Some will be gateways to profound insights. Others will continue to puzzle you. If they do, don't stop learning, but file the puzzle in the "unsolved" compartment of your mind, having committed the matter to God in prayer. Five years from now you may not understand what it was that bothered you.

HOW TO STUDY

There are several ways to study the Bible. I hope you will eventually use all of them, but to start with one or two will be sufficient. None of the methods can be divided rigidly from any other. Their boundaries overlap. Each, when used properly, tends to check the weaknesses of the others.

You can study the Bible devotionally. By this I mean that during the regular time of quiet you spend with God each day, you can meditate prayerfully on a few verses of Scripture. Whatever other form of study you adopt, do adopt this one.

It is best to follow some regular plan. Devotional reading does not mean you must switch your intellect off. It simply means your emphasis should be that of a personal application, in a spirit of reverence, of what you read.

Devotional Bible study is helpful if there are questions in your mind as you read such as:

- Is there a warning for me here?
- Is there a promise I can claim?
- Is there an example for me to follow?
- Are there commands I must obey?
- Is there a sin I must avoid or confess?
- Is there some encouragement I can take to heart?

The disadvantage of confining Bible study to devotional study is that it offers an unbalanced diet—too much milk, too little meat. It needs to be supplemented by other forms.

You can study a whole book of the Bible inductively. Inductive study is the kind where you look at a whole book in an attempt to find the basic principles it demonstrates. You ask such questions as, What are the main points the writer is making? How can I express them in my own words?

Inductive and deductive reasoning are complementary. You need both in any discipline. Too many students confine their approach to the Bible to a deductive one, saying, Since A and B are true, then according to my rule the book should say X and Y. With deductive reasoning you begin with a rule and test the material by your rule. Inductive reasoning on the other hand looks at the material to try to find *what rules arise from it.* As both kinds of reasoning have been used in understanding the Scripture, Bible students have been amazed at the unity and consistency of its teaching. But beginners should start with an inductive approach.

Inductive Bible study lays the groundwork for systematic study. It can be carried out alone or with a group of people who agree to study the same book and who can check one another's thinking. Many books have been written to teach you the principles of this kind of study, and I list some at the end of the chapter.

You can also read the Bible through from beginning to end. This is a less formidable task than you might suppose. If you read four chapters a day you will cover the material in about nine months. Use a modern translation for this sort of reading. Try it as a bedtime snack.

There are advantages in this sort of reading. You get a "bird's eye" view of a wide variety of biblical writings over a period of sixteen hundred years. You also pick up the astonishing interrelatedness of the various parts of Scripture—particularly of the Old and New Testaments. Many of the passages will become treasures as you discover them yourself for the first time. Other passages you may have to wade through.

You can also study the Bible systematically or doctrinally. By this I mean you trace a given idea through the whole Bible. You might also want to compare what you find with what scholars down the ages have written. This is by far the toughest form of study, and to my way of thinking it should not be tackled until you have a mastery of the other three methods.

TRANSLATIONS AND PARAPHRASES

English speaking Christians face a bewildering variety of translations and versions of the Bible. You can learn the history of the main Catholic and Protestant translations elsewhere. Here I will give only a general guide written from a personal point of view.

We can divide Bible translations into the following major categories:

- Older translations
- Revisions
- Personal translations
- Paraphrases
- New translations
- Translations with editorial notes and comments

The principal Protestant *older translation* is still the King James or Authorized Version. The structure of the seventeenth-century English is sonorous and beautiful. Many words have changed their meaning since the version came out. In addition there are minor errors in translation. It is worthwhile to own a copy since much Christian preaching and literature refers to this version.

Scholars have produced three different updated *revisions* of the older Authorized Version. The first, produced by British scholars in the 1880s, is known as the Revised Version. Earlier this century, North American scholars produced the American Standard Version and later the Revised Standard Version (the most readable of the three). All of these revisions are revisions of the original King James translation. They were all conducted by groups of scholars, working as teams.

By *personal translations* I mean translations made by an individual scholar. There are many of these, such as the lively J. B. Phillips translation of the New Testament or Eugene Peterson's *The Message*, though some regard these as paraphrases rather than true translations. Individual translations vary in quality with the personal biases and skill of the translator. They can have the advantage of being delightfully fresh. They can have the disadvantage of less accuracy and a more idiosyncratic bias.

Paraphrases tend to sacrifice precision in translation in the interest of intelligibility. They (for example, *The Living Bible*) are less meticulous about exactness in translation than about English semantics. They have advantage for readability but disadvantage for more careful study. The author of the paraphrase tells you what he or she thinks the verse means in lucid contemporary idiom, interpreting as well as translating. These authors know a lot more than most of us do, so their views are to be respected. But their work should be compared with more careful translations.

New translations do not attempt to update older ones. They start from scratch. Since they are more recent than some of the revisions, their authors also have access to more early documents and fragments. The New International Version and the New Revised Standard Version are new translations.

Bibles with notes. Catholics and Protestants alike have published versions of Scripture designed to promote a particular theological viewpoint by incorporating footnotes along with the text. Such Bibles should generally be avoided, not because of the view they promote but because of the mental and spiritual laziness they produce. Once you have heard an expert tell you what a passage means, you will find it easier to accept his or her opinion than to think one out for yourself. This is bad since the teachings that really stick with you are those you worked out for yourself. You might say, *Who am I to differ with an expert?* Good question. But let me remind you that even experts differ. Things are not true simply because they get into print, even if the print is on the same paper as Holy Writ.

THE TIME FACTOR
How can I find time to do all this Bible study? Christ promised

to give me rest, yet it seems all he does is to load me with extra assignments.

Not really. It is not Christ who overloads us with assignments. We overload ourselves. We perpetually take on more than we can do, then complain we are overworked. Among the things we load ourselves with are some that are good but not essential and many that are trivial and meaningless. Life becomes simpler when we wise up to the fact that we do not need to busy ourselves with two-thirds of our daily activities. Life stripped to its essentials is freedom.

And for the Christian, serious Bible study is an essential. Get rid of some nonessentials in your life and set aside a regular, weekly three-hour period for serious Bible study in addition to your daily reading.

You find time to eat, to sleep, to wash and to work. Some people also find time to attend a weekly movie or to spend hours playing games, watching TV, practicing hobbies, playing instruments, socializing, reading garbage. Find time to study the Bible. But how do I proceed? Let's say I free up three hours a week to study the Bible. What do I do then?

First, make sure that you have proper study materials. To start you will need:

- a Bible (or New Testament)
- a loose-leaf notebook

In addition it will be helpful to buy one or both of the following:

- the *New Bible Commentary*
- the *New Bible Dictionary*

Where should I begin to study? You must decide on a book to

study. If you are a new Christian, I suggest that you start with
Luke's Gospel. I feel that to start with *one* of the four Gospels is a
must. The Gospel of John was written to convince non-Christians
of Christ's deity. For that reason, while it may be good to study
John, my suggestion would be to begin with one of the other three.

Each of these three Gospels has points in its favor. The value
of all of them is that they serve to emphasize Christianity as an
historical faith. It stands or falls on events that took place in
time and space. Supremely it is centered in the life, teachings,
death and resurrection of the God-man who entered time-space
via the uterus of a peasant woman two thousand years ago.

Luke's Gospel, more than any other, is preoccupied with the
problem of sifting and analyzing all the reports surrounding the
birth, life, death and resurrection of Jesus, and with recording
as accurate an account of them as possible. For this reason I recommend it as a starting point for your serious study. But if you
have other convictions about other books in the Bible that you
want to get at first, please remember I am only suggesting.

Having collected my notebook, Bibles and commentaries,
how do I proceed? Well, if you're a serious student in other subjects, I really shouldn't have to tell you. While no real understanding of Scripture is possible apart from the Holy Spirit, the
techniques of Bible study differ from no other textual study. But
to refocus your thinking, let me remind you that your object in
any textual study is:

1. to see exactly what the text says

2. to decide what the text means

3. to explore the relevance of the text to contemporary life generally and to your own life in particular

This being so you must understand the contexts. First, you must understand the context of the whole book. By reading either the introduction to the book in the *New Bible Commentary* or the entry discussing the book in the *New Bible Dictionary*, you will learn something about the time the book was written, contemporary concerns and problems, something about the authorship, plus problems and discussions that have preoccupied previous students of the book. But only read the detailed analysis of the book in the commentary *after* your personal study of the text.

You should write brief notes from your reading to clarify your grasp of the *contextual climate* surrounding the whole book. Then you should read right through the book—not just once, but several times. Don't read with a blank mind. Read probing for answers to questions. What is the writer's purpose in writing? Why does he record the incidents he does? Is there any plan to the book or is it written haphazardly? Can it be divided into sections, and if so can titles be given to the sections? Are there any themes running through the book from beginning to end?

When you are able to answer these questions, add a further introductory section to your notes. Try at the same time to write down a very simple outline of what *you* see as its main sections and where they begin and end.

You will then be in a position to examine each section in detail, for you will have begun to understand the general context in which each paragraph, sentence and word is found. And as you do so you will keep in mind the same three basic questions: What does the passage actually say? What does it mean? How does it apply here and now? Never tackle the third question before you have answered the second. Discipline yourself to never answer the second question until you have looked the first one squarely in the face.

Many helpful books have been written on this whole subject. I only wish to let a wild, warm enthusiasm flow from my heart down my arm to flood from my pen on to the paper. Bible study has torn apart my life and remade it. That is, God, through his Word, has done so. In the darkest periods of my life, when everything seemed hopeless, I would struggle in the gray dawns of many faraway countries to grasp the basic truths of Scripture passages. I looked for no immediate answers to my problems. Only did I sense intuitively that I was drinking drafts from a fountain that gave life to my soul.

Slowly, as I grappled with textual and theological problems, a strength grew deep within me. Foundations cemented themselves to an otherworldly rock beyond the reach of time and space, and I became strong and more alive. If I could write poetry about it I would. If I could sing through paper, I would flood your soul with the glorious melodies that express what I have found. I cannot exaggerate for there are no expressions majestic enough to tell of the glory I have seen or of the wonder of finding that I, a neurotic, unstable, middle-aged man, have my feet firmly planted in eternity and breathe the air of heaven. And all this has come to me through a careful study of Scripture.

SETTING A GOAL

In my study I have experienced an ever-deepening knowledge of a person. We talk about *knowing*, but in two different senses. I can know facts. But I can also know people. Knowing facts is intellectual process. Knowing people involves emotional and volitional interactions with them.

You may read the Bible to know certain facts. But this is only the beginning. Your real aim is to know Christ. You must therefore set yourself, as you study Scripture, to get to know a person.

There are many experts on the Bible. Some will awe you by the facility with which they quote chapter and verse. Others will hint at a knowledge of the original languages. You will come across people with a formidable fund of information on any passage you could name, ready to expatiate on the subtler nuances of the biblical text at the drop of a hat.

Don't mimic them.

Knowledge, especially biblical knowledge, has the same effect as wine when it goes to your head. You become dizzily exalted. But Bible study should be conducted not with a view to knowing *about* Christ but to knowing *him* personally.

And to know Christ is to know peace. The more you know him, the less inclined you will be to impress people or to indulge in games of biblical one-upmanship. The Bible was inspired because God wants you to know him. He wants to reveal his heart to you in a love relationship. If you let him, he will make that relationship so precious that it will become a private thing that you will want to share with no one. You may be willing enough to talk about *him*. You will be glad to tell others of his goodness. But there will be secret issues between you that are between you and him alone. And he will make your life as stable as a rock and as alive as spring.

Beyond the sacred page
I seek Thee, Lord,
My spirit pants for Thee,
O living Word.[1]

A FEW SUGGESTIONS

1. Aids to Bible study

   - *New Bible Commentary.* A one-volume commentary. Helpful, provided you attempt to come to grips with the passage *before* you examine the commentary's analysis of the biblical text itself.
   - *New Bible Dictionary.* A superb tool for Bible study—really an encyclopedia on any topic in the Bible. Included are entries giving background on every book in the Bible.

2. For your own quiet time

   - Read Psalm 19. As you read, make a note of the two ways God has revealed himself to humans.
   - Verses 1-6. It is sometimes suggested that it is impossible to know anything about God apart from Scripture. What can be known from celestial bodies, and who can know it?
   - Verses 7-10. The words *law, testimony, statutes* and so forth are all used synonymously here. Make a list of what they can do for you.
   - Verses 11-14. Try repeating these verses aloud and making them your own prayer.

4

On Being a Signpost

———— 🌿 ————

They could not have looked like promising revolutionary material. That they should see themselves as deliverers of Israel was ludicrous. Their grasp of the meaning of Christ's death and resurrection was still tenuous, and their perception of their future confused.

What was going to happen on the political scene? What role would they play? Seated among the young olive trees they asked him: "Do you plan to restore Israel's sovereignty?" Many eyes were turned on him.

"None of your business!" was the effect of his retort. "That's God the Father's affair. He currently organizes the political scene. Your job will be to bear witness to me not only here, but in broadening circles throughout the earth" (see Acts 1:4-8).

Was he out of his mind? Who would believe them? What credibility would this unsophisticated group of petty misfits have in the cynical world? How much impact could they make on its tough, hostile shell?

"When the Holy Spirit has come upon you . . ."

And so it happened. Within a decade Jerusalem had been rocked to its foundations, and cities around the Mediterranean basin from Jerusalem to Rome had been stirred by feeble followers of Jesus. All the new Christians were witnesses. A few became full-fledged evangelists gifted in presenting the good news with convincing clarity and power. The two (witnesses and evangelists) worked hand in hand in the church's task of making disciples among all nations.

Today the situation remains unchanged. Every member of the worldwide church is a witness, while some have special gifts in evangelism, pastoral care and so on.

And like a witness in court, you are obliged to tell the truth, the whole truth and nothing but the truth. You will tell the truth in the sense that you are to tell what actually happened to you rather than a dressed-up version. You need neither exaggerate nor minimize what has taken place in your life or what is currently taking place. You will tell the whole truth in the sense that when there is an opportunity you will not hold anything back. You will be prepared to let your life be an open book read by all the people around you.

You will give up your right to be a private person. Just as Christ was ready to share all that he was with everyone he countered, so you will be ready to share all that he has made you with anyone you meet. You will not ram your views down anybody's throat. You will simply be open and share.

You will not only share the triumphs you have experienced but the doubts, the fears and the defeats. To do anything less would be to act as an untruthful witness. You have nothing to hide. The truth itself is infinitely more powerful than the filtered version of the truth that your vanity might prefer.

I don't know whether God will give you the gift of being an evangelist. In the general teamwork of the church, evangelists have a limited role. All of us however have the broader responsibility of bearing witness.

THE NATURE OF SIGNPOSTS

And what does it mean to bear witness? Witnesses to what? Witnesses before whom? Is a witness something you *are*, something you *say* or something you *do*? Do you wait till someone asks you for your evidence, or do you go right ahead whether they ask or not?

A witness is something you are, but what you are always determines what you say and do. The three—being, saying and doing—are part of a whole. Essentially a witness is someone *who is truthful about what he or she has seen, heard or personally experienced.* Moreover, the witness of Jesus must not only tell the truth but live it.

Two illustrations will serve to clarify. In a court of law a witness in response to questions tells the court what he or she heard, said or did. If the witness says, "I believe the prisoner was uptown that night because someone—I can't remember who it was—told me they'd seen him . . ." his testimony will be ruled inadmissible. "Did you yourself see the prisoner downtown?" is what the court wants to know. It cannot deal with a witness's conjectures or on secondhand stories.

In the same way your Christian witness must be firsthand witness. It must be about what *you* discovered when *you* read the Bible, prayed, put *your* trust in Christ or whatever.

The second illustration of witness is that of a signpost. A

signpost points to a destination. It matters little whether the signpost is pretty or ugly, old or new. It helps if the lettering is bold and clear. But the essential features are that it must point in the right direction and be clear about what it is pointing to.

If you ask people to describe the signposts that directed them to their destination, they will remember some and forget others altogether. But forgotten or remembered, the signposts will have done their job if they have got the traveler to the right place.

"You shall be witnesses unto me," Jesus told the early disciples. In a sense it matters very little whether you are an antiqued rural signpost written in elegant ancient script or a bright green modern one strung up high over the freeway. You do not exist to draw attention to yourself but to direct people's thoughts to a divine destination. A signpost has defeated its purpose if it is so attractive that it draws attention to itself rather than to a city.

Therefore remember that in witnessing, while you will be talking about your personal experience, giving as it were a first-hand report of your encounter with Christ, your witness will not focus on you but on the Christ you experience. A newly engaged fellow or girl may talk about their engagement in one of two ways. One will give a self-centered account of parties and of conquest, and will be enamored more with the state of being engaged than with the person to whom he or she is engaged; another, while confessing his or her love, will speak in glowing terms of the person who has won them. Don't be enamored with the blessed state of being a Christian, but be enamored with Christ and confess what he means to you.

Unfortunately, witnessing is not seen by many Christians as a simple telling the truth or being a signpost. It has become a complex matter focusing on technicalities of witness and on irrelevancies.

Some people "witness" by carrying leather-bound Bibles, others by giving tracts to service people or leaving literature in public toilets. Many sport bumper stickers ranging from the ancient fish symbol to "Honk if you love Jesus." Yet others erect roadside billboards. One sign near where I live reads, "The wicked will go to hell and burn forever." Some older post-Reformation groups witness by their dress. Amish and Mennonite men of certain groups do not wear ties or shave their beards, feeling it would be worldly to do so.

How can you know what true witness is? Does wearing no tie point people to Jesus? Do bumper stickers? Does bowing your head and saying grace in a restaurant?

Let me return to my original point. Witness is pointing to Jesus—not to a religious movement or even to a way of life, but to a person. A witness is someone who tells others what he or she has personally and directly discovered about Jesus and God's Word—a signpost.

So long as we fall down in our open declaration of what we personally have experienced, bumper stickers are as pointless as such things as carrying a Bible "for a testimony," unusual forms of dress and so forth. In some cases the forms of "witness" I have mentioned become misleading and self-defeating. The signpost has drawn attention to itself rather than to Jesus. The fact that the more eccentric forms of Jesus publicity give rise to derision in no way makes them Christian, however virtuous it makes the performer feel. The derision is not about Jesus but about our own kookiness. And while as kooks we may fancy ourselves persecuted for Jesus' sake, it would be more true to say that we are being laughed at because we are behaving ridiculously by human standards as well as by God's.

But before we concentrate on technicalities and specifics, let's establish the absolute necessity of witness. If you are a new Christian, do not be a secret one. The Christ who died for you demands that you confess your allegiance to him before your friends. Should you fail to do so, you will not only be acting in a manner unfaithful to Christ but will become the unhappy denizen of two worlds, feeling fully at home in neither. With your old friends you will find that the magic is gone, however hard you try to rekindle it. With your fellow Christians you will use Christian language, have a different set of jokes, shared clichés and ethical mores. With either group you may feel embarrassed when you are discovered in the company of the other.

It is not a matter of severing one set of relations in order to cement another but of being an honest person in both. The decision about what groups you belong to is not your decision. You belong to Christ. Belong to him openly and you will find that some people will reject you while others will be the more eager to welcome you.

Some people find it easy to be open. They call up their closest friends by telephone: "Listen, I've gotta talk to you. I've become a Christian. I went to this meeting, like . . . And ya know for weeks I've been . . . Listen, you must meet some of the guys." The events in their lives are turned into exuberant testimony.

Others find it hard. They choke on words like *God* and *Jesus* and *Christian*. They set out to say what they mean but beat around the bush; they use obscure words; their sentences meander in long meaningless tangles, like kittenmauled wool.

SALESMAN FOR CHRIST?

How does one witness?

I can't give you a technique. Other people might. But I don't know you. Nor do I know the people you bump into every day. Your Instructor is the Holy Spirit.

I can tell you what constitutes bad witness, however. Bad witness is insincere, and though no one wants to be insincere, many approaches to and training courses in witness unwittingly pander to our phoniness.

For instance, there are techniques based on the tacit assumption that Christ is a product for whom a market needs to be created. We must mass produce Christian packages and sell them. For some it is high-pressure salesmanship with an urgency to clinch the deal. For others it is the soft sell of "friendship evangelism." No market needs to be created. The market is already there. The fields are white unto harvest. Marketing is both the glory and the shame of Western civilization. It has been its making and will ultimately prove its undoing.

Marketers project an image. Salespeople ideally should be neat dressers, have white teeth, radiate good humor and ooze prosperity. Though they have a patter (learned under the tutelage of genial sales "coaches"), they try to be sincere by convincing first themselves, and then you, that they are doing both you and society a kindness in offering you their company's product.

In the same way we market Christ. We do it on TV and radio spots, magazine ads and above all through marketing and sales—pastors sell our "product" from pulpits and an army of lesser lights market him part time from door-to-door or wherever they can.

It would be very wrong of me to suggest that this sort of

thing is nothing more than a farce. What I am saying is that the church is in part a product of the Bible and in part of the Western free enterprise system.

Only if you understand this are you in a position to size up so many witnessing techniques. Like the salesperson, the Christian is supposed to give a good impression, dressing well and smiling "as a witness to Christ." Christians should be able, without losing their temper, to outtalk the non-Christian and corral him or her gently with words. We must beat non-Christians in sports, outperform them on the job and outshine them in brilliance. In all these ways Christians have unconsciously taken over a cultural rather than a biblical view of witness.

It is hard to do all those things—and many more—without being a phony or living under an impossible strain. For instance you can't know everything. That being so, it is inevitable that when you talk about Christ, other people will raise points you have never thought of. They may do so just to be argumentative, or they may raise a genuine difficulty from their special knowledge or their own erroneous thinking in some area you are not familiar with.

At this point you have a choice of saying, "I'm sorry. I never thought of that. I don't know how to answer your question," or you can bluff it through in an evangelistic con game in order to keep the upper hand. And to do that is to be phony.

Projecting a Christian image has pitfalls of its own. If I am sad, it may be a good exercise to look into the mirror, smile and say: *Whatever I feel like, I know that my Redeemer lives!* But to smile in order to project a joyful image when you are sick with heartache is to be phony. You will say, *But I ought not be sick at heart.* Perhaps not. But if it is wrong to be worried, it is even more wrong to try to fool people about your worry. Two sins don't add up to obedience. It would be far better to say to a non-Christian, "I know that as a Christian I should have lots of joy, but right now I don't." Witnessing and projecting an image are not the same thing.

So when you witness, do not pretend to be something you are not or to know things you don't know. *Christ may want people to discover you are weak and foolish.* He wants them to be impressed by what *he* can do in the life of a weak and foolish human being. "We have this treasure," Paul stated, "in earthen vessels, to show that the transcendent power belongs to God and not to us" (2 Cor 4:7).

I cannot emphasize too much that our job as witnesses is not to project a good image. I failed utterly to appreciate this when I was a younger Christian.

Put off by the ludicrous witness strategies of my fellow Christians, I decided to be more discreet. The result was that I became simply a nice guy. I had my sensors probing for possible areas of embarrassment and did a superb job of deflecting serious conversation, four moves in advance. But I lacked the firmness of a good diplomat. I was too busy avoiding trouble. I was much more concerned with what people thought of me rather than what they thought of Christ.

My chameleon-like skill consisted in adopting the postures and attitudes of people around me. In any verbal traffic between human beings certain matters are *assumed* to be true. If you make a flippant comment about someone, for instance, you assume that the persons you are speaking to sees life the same way you do. They may not; though chances are they will pretend they do, in which case the you are not communicating at all. You are addressing the imaginary persons you think the others are.

In my case, I would be busy adopting the mindsets and the viewpoints of the people all round me. I could laugh at their jokes without asking myself whether I really thought them funny; I could cap a cynical comment with an even more cynical one, without pausing to discover whether my own attitude was cynical or not. I was on the way to becoming a nonperson, a mere echo of other people's egos—or worse still, what *I thought* were their egos.

ON BEING REAL

In review, the essence of witnessing consists of an open declaration of truth you have experienced. A phony witness is a poor witness; an honest, open attitude is the beginning of real witness. *We find it difficult to witness because we have not learned how to be open.* This is why we feel more comfortable when we are offered easily followed techniques for witness.

I came across a book describing such techniques once. Photographs illustrated the instructions. ("Step 3b: Place your left hand on Bill's right shoulder as in illustration #4. Look him in the eye. Your manner should be confident but gentle. If he avoids eye contact say, 'Bill, look at me.' When you have good eye contact say, 'Bill, I wonder if you'll let me tell you how much Jesus means to me.'")

I'll never forget the morning I decided as far as possible to be simple and honest in my relationship with others. I made my decision with no thought of the revolution it would effect in my witness. Yet within an hour I was in serious conversation about Christ. And within twenty-four hours I had seen a man converted. I had made no conscious effort to witness or to "win a soul." Both were direct consequences of my attempt to be real.

But "being real" is hard to practice every minute of every hour. It consists of being free to express your true feelings. I say "being free" to express them to remind you that self-expression is not *a summum bonum* in life. (The perfect man is not the one who always lets us know exactly how he feels. Such a man is an insensitive boor.)

To be real does not mean you must steal when you feel covetous or murder when you feel enraged. It means being free to express ourselves when it is appropriate to do so. But we are unable to be our real selves because we are afraid. Fear seals our lips when we ought to speak, creases our faces with smiles when we are annoyed, makes us say yes when we mean no. To be real is to be free from the fears that enslave us.

Christ wants to give you that kind of freedom. God has accepted all that is behind your mask. It matters little what others think about the real you provided you can be sure of God's love. But old habits are hard to break, and if you are like me, you'll have to work on being real. It demands faith and boldness—the qualities needed to be a witness.

Why do you laugh at a dirty joke? Is it because it's funny? (Some are.) Or is it because you don't want people to think you're a wet blanket? Perhaps you don't want to embarrass the person who's telling it. Circumstances vary. No response may be necessary. If you don't think the joke is funny, don't put on a phony laugh. If some response is demanded, try, "Look, I don't want to embarrass you. I think sex is great. But it's kind of important to me. Maybe too important to joke about lightly." Your rejoinder, if it is an honest one, may pave the way to a conversation with a more serious tone.

A conversation of any kind, joking, serious, disgruntled or whatever, turns inevitably into witness if you have the courage to be yourself simply because Christ is important to you. You don't have to look for "openings." Just be you.

To be real means *being real about something and being loyal to someone.* You are to be loyal to Jesus Christ, who has become the supreme reality in your life. You are not to deny him any more than you are to do an elaborate cover-up job on your own weaknesses.

For the Christian the essence of honesty lies in being faithful not only to the truth but to the Truth. It means not denying Christ. It means that your whole life must now pivot around the commitment that he has made to you and you to him. Your every action, every thought, every word are true or false according to how they measure up to that central commitment.

HOW REAL WAS PETER?

One of the most poignant stories in the Gospels concerns Peter's stormy denial of Christ and of his subsequent restoration on the beach one early morning. Shortly before Jesus was arrested he warned his disciples of his approaching passion and predicted that Peter would deny him before dawn. Peter protested his loyalty vehemently (Lk 22:31-34). In a futile gesture to back up his protests, he perpetrated the one violent act to characterize Christ's arrest. He slashed an ear off the head of a member of the arresting party (Jn 18:10-11).

As Jesus majestically took charge of his own arrest, encouraging the frightened soldiers to take him, the disciples took to their heels. Peter and John, however, hung back and followed the arresting party. Because of John's connections in the house-

hold of the high priest, both were later admitted to the courtyard, an area crowded with the high priest's servants, a number
of soldiers and officers.

Peter may have been frightened. The whole business of following Jesus had suddenly taken a dramatic and sinister turn.
The majesty of the palace, the security and jocular ease of the
people in the courtyard would make him feel the insecurity of
his own position more keenly.

In the following hours he denied his master on three occasions (Lk 22:54-62; Jn 18:15-27). He may have excused his de-
nials as a matter of his survival and a tactic of war. He had already protested his loyalty to Jesus too strongly. Doubtless he
was struggling to maintain to himself how loyal he really was.
After all, was he not in the courtyard of his Master's enemies? Yet
at the third denial, the crowing of a cock and a simultaneous
glance from Jesus shattered his silly delusion. He suddenly saw
himself for the sentimental, weak, impetuous fool that he really
was. Overwhelmed with shame he left the courtyard and wept
bitterly.

It is impossible to know at exactly what point Peter had begun to deny Christ. Certainly in his attitude and by his actions
he must have been denying him long before he did so verbally.
The denial that sprang to his lips at the first accusation must already have been present in his demeanor. He was playing a part
in which he fooled himself and tried to fool people around him.
The need to be liked remained in his character for as long as history records. And it is our own need to be liked that causes us
by a thousand subtle gestures to deny Christ today. Much of my
own flippancy was precisely that sort of denial. It was a cover
up for my embarrassing relationship to Jesus Christ.

Peter loved Christ and so did I. Like a man torn between his mistress and his wife, Peter loved two things at the same time, the admiration of other people and the presence of his Master. It was an uncomfortable situation to be in. Neither mistresses nor wives are willing to give in to one another. As a jealous spouse Christ wants and claims absolute loyalty from his followers. And that means that by every action, every thought, every word you must be loyal to him and not conceal your loyalty.

So at the heart of witness lies integrity in a personal relationship. If you would be a faithful witness, turn your thoughts constantly to God. Let it become your habit in every encounter with other people and as you turn to every activity to say, "Lord, I am nothing but your blood-bought servant. Help me to behave as such now."

Be courteous. Don't make it your aim to impress others by the brilliance of your repartee. Don't try to be the center of attention or the monopolizer of the conversation. Aim rather at putting others at their ease. Don't pretend to know things you don't know. If you argue, try to understand what the other person is saying. You should not try to win a verbal fencing match so much as to understand and be understood.

If you are real, your actions and words will match. You will find yourself glad to perform acts of courtesy and consideration for a roommate, for family members. You will be less inclined to borrow and more prompt to return or to lend to others. You will be more punctual at handing in assignments. You will be less of a grouch. You will not suddenly become perfect. But when you behave badly, you will recognize that an apology is owed and make the apology. Where you don't find yourself behaving generously, God will show you and you will be grieved. You will be willing to own up to your weakness to God, to other Christians and to non-Christians. And if someone compliments you on your character, you will not say: "Aw shucks, it's nothing," but "Thanks. I haven't always been that way though. I used to be quite different."

HOSTILE REACTIONS

There have been times in history when a tyrant would lop off the heads of any messengers who brought him bad tidings. Peter was facing more than ridicule. He was in danger of his life. People around you are not likely to be quite so hostile when you talk about Christ, yet not all will respond positively. The Greek word translated "witness" in the New Testament is the word from which we derive our English word *martyr*. Such was the persecution early Christians encountered that witnessing and martyrdom become two sides of the same coin. It is possible that during our own lifetime in the West the same may happen again.

People's reactions to learning of Christ have ranged from murderous, paranoid hatred to eager, glad acceptance. Sometimes it has provoked nothing more than mild amusement or interested curiosity.

You must recognize beforehand that people will sometimes react strongly. If you are unprepared, you may feel that *you* are to blame for what has happened, whereas it may have nothing to do with you at all.

I remember a violent reaction to a remark I made to a psychiatrist who was supervising part of my residency training. He was treating a homosexual patient by teaching him in easy stages how to date and how to make love to girls—in fact how to seduce them. I commented that my religious convictions would make it difficult for me to use the same method. His face flushed with anger and he spat contempt at me.

Had that incident taken place a few years previously, I would have been filled with anxiety and guilt, wondering where I had gone wrong. As it was I merely made a mental note that my supervisor had hang-ups in the areas of religion and sex. Dismissing it with a shrug of my shoulders, I continued to be completely open with him about the Christian convictions I had.

Remember: People will react to you. A favorable reaction does not mean you are witnessing skillfully any more than a hostile reaction means that you have blown it. By all means be self-critical and check to see whether you have not been tactless, rude, critical, discourteous or opinionated. However, the reaction may tell you something not about yourself but about the person to whom you are bearing witness.

A hostile reaction is to be welcomed. It may be a sign that you have prodded a sore spot. No one could have displayed a more diabolical ferocity against Christian witness than Saul of Tarsus; yet his very fury was a measure of his own desperate struggle with his conscience. "It is hard for you to kick against the goads" was Christ's apt comment (Acts 26:14 NASB).

If you *know* that strong reactions are to be welcomed, you will be less likely to fall into the trap of getting angry yourself or of becoming defensive or argumentative. The Holy Spirit will give you both compassion and perceptiveness for those who so react.

A strong reaction may take the form of criticism against you or Christians generally. Words like *hypocrisy, unscientific* and *escapism* may bombard you. My reaction as a psychiatrist is usually one of, "You seem to feel pretty strongly about this. Why?" I don't suggest you copy me, but I do urge you not to fall into the trap of defending the actions and attitudes of your fellow Christians or yourself.

In telling what Christ has done for you, you are not being called on to justify the Crusades, or twenty-first-century Christian materialism any more than you can justify the failure and sin of many Christian groups. A more appropriate response in such situations might follow the lines of, "Yes. A good many evil things have been done in the name of Christianity. But are the Crusades really what keep you from believing that Christ is alive?"

THE NEED TO KNOW MORE

Many of us would feel more secure if we could memorize a set speech and trot it out like a salesman. At least one Christian organization encourages its members to write out the story of their conversion, memorize it and then use it whenever they have an opportunity.

I have already objected to such a procedure on moral grounds. I would add the criticism that no two personal encounters are the same and that to repeat the same words in every encounter involves the risk of being insensitive to the real needs of the person I am talking to.

In part then I have been saying: Tell it like it is by responding honestly and naturally to the person you are with. Be loyal to Christ moment by moment and the words will look after themselves.

However, I must add a caveat. Honesty will at times compel you to admit your ignorance of certain aspects of your faith. There is no reason to be ashamed of not knowing everything, but neither is there any good reason to remain ignorant about your faith. Make it your lifelong task to have a growing grasp of the basis of your faith. Become an expert in it. Don't be satisfied with memorizing a few proof texts, but get a grasp of "the whole counsel of God," in order that you may become able to give a clear account of why you believe what you believe.

Begin today. Make use of your quiet time as well as group Bible study. Honesty and ignorance don't have to be married. Your knowledge must not be allowed to make you conceited or to play one-upmanship with people you talk to. But you must seek earnestly to "always be prepared to make a defense to any one who calls you to account for the hope that is in you, yet do it with gentleness and reverence" (1 Pet 3:15). We are instructed "in malice . . . be children, but in understanding be men" (1 Cor 14:20 KJV).

SUMMARY

You are a witness whether you want to be one or not. Either you are a good witness or a poor one.

A good witness tells the truth about what he or she has personally discovered. In doing so the witness acts like a signpost pointing others to Christ.

Witnessing techniques are to be used with caution. They are never a substitute for personal honesty or for the power of the Holy Spirit.

The task of a witness is not to convert people nor to "clinch a deal" but to supply them with the data through which the Holy Spirit brings conviction.

To supply them with adequate data you will need to add to your personal experience a comprehensive grasp of why you believe what you believe.

A PASSAGE TO STUDY

Read John 4:1-30, 39-42.

1. Some people say Jesus sat on the well in order to get a chance of talking to the woman. What evidence is there in the passage to support or to undermine this hypothesis?

2. At the sixth hour (v. 6) the sun is high. It has been suggested that Jesus' request for water was an opening evangelistic gambit. The evidence is less conclusive here, but do you think his request arose from thirst or as a stratagem? Give your reasons.

3. Verses 9, 19-20. How did Jesus respond to the woman's argument?

4. Verses 29-30, 41-42. Notice and comment on the relationship in the making of converts between (1) the woman's words of testimony and (2) the word of Christ. How can the lesson apply to your own witness?

5

His Infernal Majesty

I stated in chapter one that your relationship with the evil one has changed.

You may not have realized you had a relationship with him at all (unless you were fooling around with the occult). Yet aware of it or not, his spirit was at work in your body (Eph 2:2). Unknown to you, his deceptions obscured your thinking while his music inflamed your senses and influenced your will. He thought of himself as your master, but like credit rating agencies he made himself as unobtrusive as possible. His greatest skill lay in giving you the feeling that you were your own master.

C. S. Lewis's remark that humanity falls into two equal and opposite errors concerning the devil is now more famous than the book *(The Screwtape Letters)* in which it is found. The errors, according to Lewis, consist either in taking the devil altogether too seriously or in not taking him seriously enough. The devil welcomes a Hume or a Faust with equal zest. He is equally delighted by an atheist, a liberal theologian or a witch. And he feels as happy with a Christian whose mind is preoccupied with demons all day long as he is with one who never gives them a thought.

But he is living and virulent. His supreme object is to hurt Christ and Christ's cause. You personally are of no interest to him. It is only as you relate to Christ that you assume significance in his eyes. Before you became a Christian he was mainly interested in blinding you to the truth of Christ or perhaps in seducing you further into his terrain. But this was not because of your personal importance. He only used you to get back at God. Similarly, now that you are a Christian his interest in you has nothing to do with you as an individual so much as with your potential for Christ's cause. To God you are very important. But to Satan you are nothing more than a potentially useful microbe.

He and his hellions will damage you along one or more of four lines: They will *tempt*, *accuse*, *deceive* and *devour*.

TEMPTATION WITHOUT DISMAY

You will be tempted. The kinds of temptation may change: Candies for kids, sensuality for the young, riches for the middle aged and power for the aging. The evil one can ring the changes with greater skill than any advertising agency.

You will be tempted continuously. You will be tempted ferociously at times of crisis. Jesus himself was tempted "in all points as we are" (that is, to commit adultery, to steal, to lie, to kill, etc.) *"yet without sin."*

Therefore temptation itself need not dismay you. It was your Savior's lot and it will be yours. As long as you live you will be tempted. But if temptation is no cause for dismay, it is likewise no excuse for sin. Nowhere in Scripture are we justified by pray-

ing, "Lord it's true I sinned, but you see the devil tempted me."
This was the first prayer of confession in the Garden of Eden
("The serpent tricked me and I ate" [Gen 3:13 NEB]), and it
didn't wash with God. James is contemptuous of any attempt by
a Christian to slough off personal responsibility for sin. "Each
person is tempted when he is lured and enticed *by his own desire*.
Then desire when it has conceived gives birth to sin" (Jas 1:14-
15 italics added).

There is no inconsistency between James's view that temptation is a person's inner lusts and the view that he or she is lured
by satanic appeal.

Have you ever fooled around with a piano? Open the top.
Press the loud pedal. Then sing a note into the piano as loudly
as you can. Stop and listen. You will hear at least one cord vi-
brating in response to the note you sang. You sing—and a string
in the piano picks up your voice and plays it back.

Here then is a picture of temptation. Satan calls and you vibrate. The vibration is the "lust" James speaks of. Your desire is
to go on responding to his call. There is nothing bad about vi-
brating. The cord was made to vibrate and to vibrate powerfully.
But it was meant to vibrate in response to a hammer—not in response to a voice.

The appropriate response, then, is not to vibrate rapturously
to the voice of the devil but to release the loud pedal and close
the top of the piano. As Luther put it quaintly, you cannot stop
birds flying above your head, but you can prevent them from
building a nest in your hair.

In more concrete terms, whether vibration consists of sexual
arousal, angry feelings, a desire to possess something beautiful
or whatever, *the vibration itself is not evil.* Sexual arousal has its

place. The question is under what circumstances? Or again, is *this* the appropriate object and *this* the appropriate occasion? If not, slam down the lid of the piano and get your big foot off the loud pedal.

While there exists an infinite variety of notes the devil can whistle, his temptations fall under three broad groupings: the lust of the flesh, the lust of the eye and the pride of life.

Put in modern terms, these groupings refer to a basic problem in Christian living. A *desire* may be your servant; a *lust* is your master. The lust of the flesh means to be dominated by your physical appetites: hunger, thirst, the need for sleep, the desire for sex or for physical exercise. Obviously physical appetites are wholesome. Generally they are meant to be satisfied. But we live in an age when eating, drinking and "the great sexual experience" are presented to us as goals in themselves. People bow down and worship them. They live to eat or to copulate, instead of accepting food and sex with gratitude and in their proper place.

The lust of the eye means to have your life governed by a love of beautiful things whether you conceive of beauty in terms of a Maserati, a black tulip or an original Picasso. There is nothing wrong with liking or wanting beautiful things. God is a God of beauty. But the passion to possess and hoard beauty is a lust that can destroy Christian living.

The pride of life has mainly to do with ambition. Again, ambition is good. God implants in our beings the desire to excel. But excellence too can become a tyrant, dominating our whole view of life. I may excuse excessive ambition as wanting to excel "for Christ" when the real inner need is to excel to prove something of myself. You must do serious thinking about your ambitions and ask yourself, *Is ambition my master or my servant?*

The three lusts—of the flesh, of the eye and of ambition—correspond to three psychological responses Eve gave to the primal satanic temptation. "The woman saw that the tree was good for food [the lust of the flesh], and that it was a delight to the eyes [the lust of the eye], that the tree was to be desired to make one wise [the pride of life]" (Gen 3:6).

They also call to mind Satan's three-pronged attacks on our Savior: " 'Command this stone to become bread' [the lust of the flesh]. . . . 'Throw yourself down' [the pride of life]. . . . The devil took him up, and showed him all the kingdoms of the world in a moment of time, . . . It shall all be yours' [the lust of the eye and the pride of life]" (Lk 4:3, 9, 5, 7).

Yet we should not concern ourselves with the form of temptation but with how to resist it. Let me be very simple. Satan tempts *from behind*. "Look," he whispers, "Isn't it beautiful? Just think what you could do . . . what people would say . . . how you would be admired . . . how much power you would have . . . look, *look,* Look!" The Bible gives us two complementary counsels about temptation, one on temptation itself and the other on the tempter. Concerning temptation we are simply told: Flee temptation. Concerning the tempter the word is: Resist the devil, *and he will flee from you.*

Think how these two counsels work together. Did you ever run away from something and face it at the same time? How could you?

Never face temptation. Flee from it. And in fleeing, *turn* your back on it. And in turning, whom will you face? Who has been standing behind you and whispering vivid word pictures in your ear? Turn and face him. Resist him. And his satanic majesty will withdraw.

But how do you resist?

Well, turning is three-quarters of the battle. Later we will discuss what Paul calls "the whole armor of God." For the present let me confine myself to one piece of that armor which he calls "the sword of the Spirit . . . the Word of God."

Many commentators have pointed out that when Jesus was tempted in the wilderness he responded to each satanic suggestion with the words, "it is written . . . it is written . . . it is written." Each time that Jesus employed the sword of the Spirit, he slashed the tempter.

Many Christians have testified to the astonishing effect particular Scriptures have in their ability to cope with temptation. The Bible is called the sword of the Spirit for three reasons: The Spirit inspired it; the Spirit will place it in your hands and teach you skill in using it; the Spirit will make it cut deep. Therefore get to know Scripture. And as you turn your back on temptation and face your tempter, reach out your hand for the sword that the Spirit puts in your grasp. Then plunge it deep into the tempter and hear him howl in pain as he flees back to hell from before a "microbe with an Achilles' heel."

ACCUSATION OF THE BRETHREN

Oh, how he loves to accuse you! "Now the salvation and the power and the kingdom of our God and the authority of his Christ have come, for the accuser of our brethren has been thrown down, who accuses them day and night before our God" (Rev 12:10).

He accuses. Accuses whom? He accuses the brethren; that is

to say all Christians. He accuses *you*. To this day he tries to ape the counsel for the crown.

Where does he accuse? He accuses you "before our God." When you kneel to pray, his accusations will echo through the vault of your skull. When you seek to bear witness to Jesus, he will scream to God of your vile unworthiness, and if ever you try to preach in public—watch out! He will rant and rave before God in your hearing about the foulness of the lips that attempt to preach God's Word.

When does he accuse? He accuses day and night. As you wake for a moment in the night, he will still be accusing. In your dreams he will accuse. You will drink your morning coffee with a tablespoonful of denunciation and do your day's work against a background of accusation muzak.

So naturally you will feel guilty, which will take the sparkle out of your eye and the snap out of your step. Guilt feelings will dull the edge of your witness, take the heart out of Christian service and make any public testimony as stale as moldy fish. And this is precisely what Satan has in mind. Accusation is his secret weapon, supremely effective in taking the zap out of the Christian army's attack. How could guilt-ridden soldiers possibly assail the gates of hell?

"But hold on," you say. "Does guilt not arise from sin, and shouldn't sin always be confessed?" To the second part of your question: Yes. Sin should always be confessed and where necessary, restitution should be made. There will always be sin to confess (1 Jn 1:8-9). But to the first part of your question: No. Guilt does not always imply sin.

Psychoanalysts speak of neurotic guilt, guilt feelings that arise because of our early experiences. In doing so they are trying to explain why we feel guilty. But their theories raise serious questions: Do feelings of guilt necessarily mean I have sinned? Is *felt* guilt *true* guilt? Can consciences always be trusted? These issues are of paramount importance. Satan has no power to paralyze the hosts of heaven with true guilt. (Christ's death is sufficient to take care of that.) False guilt is the weapon he uses most. And false guilt means *feeling guilty when I have no reason to*. It is accuser-induced guilt. The late Dr. Donald Grey Barnhouse frequently gave a brilliant illustration of the limitations of conscience. Conscience, he used to tell us, is like a sundial.

A sundial only works when there is light. It does not work at midnight in a fog. Moreover it requires light from the proper source. The moon makes it point to the wrong time. Take a flashlight with you and walk around a sundial at 3 a.m. It will tell you whatever time you want. Conscience, likewise, functions only when it has the light of God's Word illuminated by God's Spirit shining on it.

When psychoanalysts raise the question of false guilt, they are raising a perfectly biblical point. We may disagree with them as to the *content* of false guilt, but about the existence of the phenomenon they are right on the ball.

In *The Holy War* John Bunyan describes the capture of the town of Mansoul by Apollyon's forces. A principal citizen of Mansoul was Mr. Conscience, the town crier. It was the duty of Mr. Conscience to warn Mansoul of danger and to announce celebrations and glad tidings.

Following the city's capture by Prince Apollyon, the town crier became insane. Peril might loom over the city yet Mr. Conscience would remain wrapped in moody silence in his watchtower. Yet in the night while all slept he would shriek his crazy warning of nonexistent ills or sing insanely of joys that were not to be.

All this was Bunyan's graphic way of telling us that the conscience of the fallen human has gone awry. It can live in comfort with some sin yet be unbelievably sensitive about things that are not sin at all. Nor are matters automatically rectified when a person becomes a Christian. Certainly his or her conscience is quickened, but wrong training from the past still interferes with its proper functioning.

How then may I distinguish right from wrong? How may I rid myself of the appalling burden *of false* guilt? How may I know the difference between the accusations of Satan and the conviction of the Holy Spirit?

I suppose there is a long-range answer and a short-range answer in the matter of conscience and its proper functioning. The long-range answer has to do with Scripture. Day by day, week by week, year by year my conscience must be reinstructed, reoriented by a progressive knowledge of God's Word. Just as the compass in a sailing boat must be "swung," that is, rechecked and modified while the boat is made to face in every direction, so over the years a Christian's conscience becomes ever more finely and accurately tuned as practical experience in Scripture is gained under the Spirit's tutelage. All the while our behavior must be modified by what we learn from Scripture. We must sail according to the corrected compass.

Yet the short-range answer is every bit as important and will remain so to the end of your days. The Spirit convicts; the enemy accuses. How may I know which voice is which?

Think of it logically for a moment.

What is the enemy trying *to do* when he accuses? And the

Spirit when he convicts? Clearly the enemy seeks to *destroy* your fellowship with God. The Spirit, on the other hand, is attempting to *restore* your fellowship with God. (And note that the accuser often tells the truth. The sins and failures he accuses me of are not always false.)

Now if the Spirit is attempting to *restore* your fellowship with God, it follows that when sin is confessed, conviction will melt away and the blossom of fellowship burst out with new fragrance. It also follows that if Satan is bent on *destroying* your fellowship with God and if your sense of sin results from satanic accusation, then no such fragrance will be experienced. It will seem to you rather that your confession has somehow been inadequate, that you need to be more thoroughgoing in your analysis of your sin, more rigorous in your restitution. Yet to your dismay the confession is never thoroughgoing enough. "What was your *real* motive in that 'good' deed?" a voice will ask. "Are you *sure* you have left nothing out? Can't you *sense* that you're only skimming the surface? Don't you see how deceit permeates your heart like a vile poison?" In horror you will recoil at the ever-broadening vision of your own evil. First grayness, then blackness will envelop you as a cloud, and you will sit in huddled, shivering misery wrapped in the center of your own cold shadow. The accuser will have achieved his objective.

Now the only place in Scripture where the devil is actually *named* "the accuser" is in Revelation 12:10. In the very next sentence, we read that the brethren "conquered him by the blood of the Lamb."

Much nonsense has been talked and much tomfoolery acted out around the sacred words "the blood of Jesus."

Let it be understood that the words have no magic in them.

They do not constitute a spell. They should never be used as an incantation. It may be true that the response to the words "the blood of Jesus" can indeed be dramatic. Hobgoblins and foul fiends are jumpy creatures.

But in reference to the accuser their meaning is precise. Blood in Scripture *always* symbolizes death, and usually violent or sacrificial death. ("His blood be upon us and upon our children," "the avenger of blood" and so forth.) Even where it seems to speak of life, it speaks of it only as life poured out in death. So when John says that the brethren overcame the accuser by the blood of the Lamb, he is really telling us that they overcame his accusations by the death of Christ.

The second thing you must understand about blood is that it was given to *cleanse our consciences*. In hymnology we sing about our hearts being washed in the blood of Jesus. The tunes may be musical but the theology grates. "For if the sprinkling of defiled persons with the blood of goats and bulls . . . sanctifies," writes the author of Hebrews, "how much more shall the blood of Christ . . . purify your conscience from dead works to serve the living God" (Heb 9:13-14).

Try to understand the verse. All along we have been considering the satanic strategy of destroying your fellowship with God by creating a guilty conscience in you. God's answer to your guilty conscience is the death of his Son. *Your* answer to a guilty conscience is usually something you *do*, like confessing harder, praying more, reading your Bible, paying more than your tithe in the offering and so on. These actions are what the writer to the Hebrews calls "dead works," the very things your conscience needs to be cleansed from and the very things that eventually get you wrapped up in the black shadow of your own guilt.

Consider another verse in Hebrews: "Let us draw near with a true heart in full assurance of faith, with our hearts sprinkled clean from an evil conscience and our bodies washed with pure water" (Heb 10:22). There you have it. Water for the body but blood for the conscience. And notice the context.

Do you know how to go *boldly* into the presence of God the holy One? Or do you find yourself creeping into his presence, head down and shoulders slumped? The difference between the two approaches has to do with your conscience. Someone with a clean conscience runs into God's presence, arms widely spread, like a child leaping into the embrace of his or her father. Is that how you come?

Do you not understand? The Father does not welcome you because you have been trying hard, because you have made a thoroughgoing confession or because you have been making spiritual strides recently. He does not welcome you because you have something you can be proud about. He welcomes you because *his Son died for you*. His breast has always yearned for you and his arms yearned to enfold you. Christ's death has now made it possible for the Father to do what he wanted to do all along. So come boldly—sprinkled by blood. Let him enfold you to the warmth of his bosom while his hot tears wash over your body.

Hot tears? Does the expression sound irreverent or sentimental? I have no words that do justice to the love that led to the death of God's Son. The universe ought to have stopped in its tracks, and I am sorry it didn't. No more heinous crime was ever committed against God nor a greater act of love consummated on behalf of the criminal. Are you blasphemous enough to suppose that your dead works, your feeble efforts can add to the finished work of a dying Savior? "It is finished!" he cried.

Completed. Done. Forever ended. He crashed through the gates of hell, set prisoners free, abolished death and burst in new life from the tomb. All to set you free from sin and open the way for you to run into the loving arms of God.

Now do you understand how "our brethren" overcame the accuser by the blood of the Lamb? *They refused to let his accusations impede their access to God.* A simple confession was enough. They faced the accuser boldly saying, "We already know the worst you could ever tell us and so does God. What is more the blood of Jesus is enough."

> Well may the Accuser roar
> Of ills that I have done:
> I know them all, and thousands more:
> Jehovah knoweth none![1]

Therefore when you find the gray cloud descending—as you pray, work, testify or whatever—look up to God and say, "Thank you my Father for the blood of your Son. Thank you even now that you accept me gladly, lovingly in spite of all I am and have done—because of his death. Father and God, I come."

Say it to him now. Say it sitting, kneeling or standing. Do not wait a moment. Your heavenly Father is waiting for you. He misses you. He bids you come. Now. Sprinkled by blood.

DECEPTION OVERCOME

But the believers of Revelation 12 also overcame Satan by the word of their testimony. There, Satan is described in three roles. He is the accuser. He is also "that ancient serpent . . . the deceiver of the whole world." And he is described as a dragon devouring and making war (referred to elsewhere as the "roaring lion").

Christians overcome Satan, the deceiving serpent, by the "word of their testimony." In doing so they launch their warfare into enemy-held territory. Freed from a sense of guilt and therefore ready to do battle with a single mind, they launch an attack on the satanic darkness with penetrating rays of light.

"The deceiver of the whole world" began by deceiving Eve.

Did God really say that? Well now, he was hardly speaking the truth. The fact of the matter is . . .

And millions of Eve's descendants have been falling for the ploy ever since. Paul describes Satan as "the God of this world [who] hath blinded the minds of them which believe not, lest the light of knowledge . . ." (2 Cor 4:4 KJV). Blinded minds. Deceived hearts. Deceived through TV ads and university educations. Use pink toilet paper and you'll be happy. Buy a shiny car and a pretty lady will get in it. Invest in real estate and insurance and you'll be safe. Smell nice and bed nice. Sex makes you fulfilled. Get good grades and corporations will love you. Money isn't everything, but . . .

Talk sociological gobbledygook and people will bow before your wisdom. Let's all learn to accept death without the need of superstitious fantasies of what lies beyond. Science says there is no God. Science says there is a God. Science says Genesis is true, so it must be. It's amazing what science will prove. Let us therefore bow down to the latest hypothesis. Let us kneel before our transactional analyst.

Does it all sound too ridiculous to credit? Know then that Satan the deceiver understands his business well. Anyone who can keep you feverishly hunting for the perfect deodorant without letting you realize what an ass you are is supremely competent.

And if you think that words alone, my words or anyone else's words, will undeceive the blinded minds of "them that believe not," you are a fool. I can make people smile momentarily at their idiocy by my verbal skill, but they'll go right on hunting for the perfect deodorant.

No, it is by "the word of [your] testimony" that you will overcome the deceiver. And that means the Word of God that has been proved true by you in your experience and about which you may legitimately testify. Once you are able to say, "The Bible says . . . and it was such a help to me that it really solved my problem," the gates of hell will not prevail against you. The light of your words will pierce the satanic blindness of people around you, and they will begin to see. And when that happens the dragon will swish his powerful tail and sweep a third of heavenly bodies into blackness. He will rage and gnash his teeth, for he will know that his end is nearer. Microbes with Achilles' heels will assume a greater importance to him.

WARFARE WITH THE DEVOURER

"Be strong in the Lord and in the strength of his might" (Eph 6:10).

What chance does a microbe have against Satan? What chance did Bunyan's Christian have against Apollyon? Of what use will *you* be in a battle with the legions of hell?

Please notice: You will be part of the attacking force. If the passage in Ephesians sounds like advice for *defense,* it is defense against *counterattack.* Once you are committed to giving the word of your testimony you are part of Christ's attacking army. You are invading enemy-held territory.

But being part of Christ's army entitles you to all of heaven's resources. The might of Jehovah is at your disposal. So be strong *in the Lord*.

"Good advice," you may say, "but in concrete terms how may I be strong *in the Lord?*" You may be so by having no confidence in your own ability, by doing what God says and trusting him to back you, by exercising what is called "the obedience of faith," by stepping, at God's command, toward closed glass doors and watching them swing open as you reach them. Your strength lies in what *he* does when *you* obey.

Yet the counterattack will come against you. So you will need armor, for the principalities and powers will send their legions to assail you. "Put on the whole armor of God" so that their counterattack will fail. Armor against what? Against cunning and trickery. To be sure the metaphor is mixed, but get your Bible out and open it at Ephesians 6:10-18. Let's look at each piece of equipment the passage mentions.

What kind of armor will resist *cunning?* Well, you begin with the belt of *truth* (v. 14). Basic to all your defense must be an accurate perception of the way things really are. Reality, for our purposes, may be defined as *things the way God sees and reveals them*.

The breastplate of righteousness is a metaphorical alternative for a blood-sprinkled conscience. Your defense against the spear thrust of accusation is the solid assurance that the Father accepts you completely because of the death of the Son. To put on the breastplate of righteousness is another way of saying to overcome by the blood of the Lamb.

I am a little uncertain about the military footwear Paul recommends (v. 15). Commentaries differ. It sounds as though he is saying you should get a solid footing in your grasp of the Christian gospel. But the "shield of faith" (v. 16) is straightforward enough. Whatever flaming darts—of fear, of dismay, of pain—may be flung at you, catch them with a bold affirmation of your confidence in Christ. He is alive. He is in control. Look up to him and tell him you will trust him come what may, and the flaming darts will sputter and die.

The helmet of salvation (v. 17) has to do with Christian hope (see 1 Thess 5:8). It is fashionable in psychiatry to stress the importance of the "here-and-now." Who cares what happened when I was three years old? What does it matter where I will be in ten years? It's *now* that matters.

And so it is. But we must not be too hasty to dump past and future into the garbage can. To the Christian the past matters intensely and the future does too. The here-and-now can only be *understood* in the light of the past and only *faced* in the light of the future. Life without hope is death in the here-and-now.

And Christ gives you hope. Present chaos will not endure. There is cosmic hope of a restitution of all things. Christ will judge and restore. There is personal hope. You will take part in that same restoration. Don't live *in* the future but work for it, and your skull will be well protected.

So when the counterattack comes, stand with all the firmness of a true believer. Pray unceasingly but pray on your feet. And the counterattack, however fierce, will suddenly die away. What happened to Christ will happen to you. The enemy will depart and leave you alone for a little while (Lk 4:13).

At least he will almost always do so. I must not leave you with the false impression that there are no casualties in the battle. Let me remind you of the four roles that Satan has in his opposition to Christ. He is the tempter, the accuser, the deceiver and the devourer. When he neither tempts you nor stops you from bearing witness by incapacitating you with guilt, you will find yourself encountering him as the deceiver of the whole world. And once you start to overcome him by the word of your testimony, he will henceforth assume mainly the roles of the roaring lion and the devouring dragon.

Let me be clear what I am talking about. Satan is not now trying to devour your soul but to kill or maim your body. God usually doesn't let him. But again we are not engaged in play war but in a real one. Christ himself was crucified battling to conquer death and hell and to rise again.

Paradoxically, it is in his role as the devouring dragon that we see Satan's hopeless weakness. When he kills someone, he has reached the nadir of frustration and hopelessness. Christ in his death won his greatest victory.

> He hell, in hell, laid low;
> Made sin, He sin o'erthrew;
> Bow'd to the grave, destroyed it so;
> And death, by dying, slew.[2]

When we say that martyr blood is the seed of the church, we are not whitewashing tragedy with a sentimental cliché but stating a simple fact. When Ayore Indians bludgeoned five New Tribes missionaries to death in the Bolivian jungle in the early 1940s, there arose, even during wartime in the United States, a tremendous surge of new missionary interest. The five were replaced by fifty. There is now a growing Ayore church.

When a couple of decades later another five independent missionaries were murdered by Huaorani (Auca) Indians in Ecuador, the same thing happened. Missionary work among primitive tribal people has not been the same since.

Let me state it in simple terms. Satan cannot hurt you until your task for Christ is completed. Until that time comes you are truly immortal. He may roar. He may threaten. But he is powerless.

When your earthly task is completed, it is possible that he may kill you. But you will achieve by your death more than by your life. *Satan is powerless to stop the advance of the gospel through your life.*

Running through this chapter as a leitmotif has been the motto of Cambridge Inter-Collegiate Christian Union in Britain. It is the verse I quoted earlier: Revelation 12:11. Let me summarize what I have been saying.

It seems to me that in this verse "our brethren" overcame Satan in three ways. They overcame him as the accuser by the blood of the Lamb. They overcame him as the deceiving serpent by the word of their testimony. And they overcame him as the devouring dragon because they loved not their lives unto the death.

Such people are invincible. Nothing can stop them, and nothing ever will.

And tho this world, with devils filled,
Should threaten to undo us;
We will not fear, for God hath willed
His truth to triumph through us: . . .
Let goods and kindred go,
This mortal life also;
The body they may kill:
God's truth abideth still,
His Kingdom is forever.[3]

A PASSAGE TO STUDY

Read Ephesians 6:10-20.

1. The passage begins with the word *Finally.* Skim through Ephesians 4:25—6:9 to get the general drift of the context of the passage.

2. Why would Paul bother to say that we are not contending with flesh and blood (v. 12)? What bearing does the statement have on our relations with (1) non-Christians, (2) fellow Christians, (3) members of our family?

3. What general area of the body is offered no protection by any of the armor mentioned—even by a shield? Is it possible to draw inferences from this absence of protection?

4. Of how much importance is prayer in the battle? How able are you personally to carry out verse 18?

6

Faith

———— ❦ ————

Faith is at the core of practical Christianity. Your Christian life began when you began to believe. It has grown and will grow as faith widens the channel along which grace flows to you. No aspect of your Christian life is of greater importance.

Yet few aspects of Christian living cause more confusion. "Lord, increase our faith," the disciples pleaded, only to be told that faith the size of a grain of mustard seed was all that was required for the most momentous tasks (Mt 17:20). Yet if so little was needed, why was their experience so poor?

Clearly, before we can answer questions of this nature, we need to understand what faith is.

A HUMAN RESPONSE TO GOD'S INITIATIVE

Faith is a person's response to God's initiative. Your first faith was the positive response you made to the Holy Spirit when he brought truth about Christ home to your heart. As God's light dawned on you, you decided to bow your will to Christ and to entrust your destiny to him. You could have responded negatively. The choice was yours. But the process, which was to lead either to rejection or acceptance, began with God.

When the angel appeared to the virgin Mary to announce her awesome responsibility, she responded humbly with "Let it be to me according to your word" (Lk 1:38). Very few Protestant writers have commented on how much faith Mary had at this point. Yet two things are clear: First, her faith was her response to the Word of God coming to her, and second, through her faith God invaded history.

To realize that faith is your response to something God does or says will take pressure off you and enable you to adopt a more constructive attitude to it. Don't look inside yourself and ask, *How much faith do I have?* Look to God and ask, What are you saying to me? What would you have me do? When Jesus praised the great faith of different men and women in the Gospels, he was not praising a mystical inner state. He was usually commenting on a concrete action by which someone responded to him. It might have been the action of the Roman centurion who sent his servants to Christ asking only that Christ speak the word of power, or the pathetic struggle of a feeble woman to touch his robe. Whatever it was, it was the person's response, usually in overt action, to God's call.

Once you understand this, you will also begin to see why the amount of faith you have is a less crucial issue than you might have thought. The saying of Jesus about the grain of mustard seed begins to make sense.

How much faith does it take for a nonswimmer to push off the side? Only enough to transfer the support of his body for a fraction of a second from the side of the pool to the water.

How much faith did Martha need to get Lazarus back from the dead? Precious little (Jn 11:38-40). If we are to go by mystical inner states, every evidence points to Martha having no faith at all. No, what she needed was *enough faith* to give orders for the tombstone to be moved, in spite of the doubts she felt. And Lazarus was raised from the dead.

Actions in most of us involve decision. I see the elevator door open, and I decide to get in. I know that last time when I punched button 15 I went up to the fifteenth floor. So I decide to punch the button again.

Faith then is your decision to respond to God's Word. The decision may either manifest itself in some outward action or else in what we might call an "interior action"—like the committing of your eternal destiny into the hands of Christ. In time the decision grows into an attitude, an attitude of always being ready to respond positively to God's Word.

When I was younger and more absorbed in faith-science tensions in my studies, I used to point out that faith is a decision or an attitude *based on evidence* (the historical evidence contained in the Judeo-Christian documentation). What I said was true, but my vision was limited. I failed then to see that whereas the scientist looks actively for evidence, the Christian has it trumpeted in his ear all day long. God is active in speaking, in revealing, in bringing his Word to my heart. Therefore I now prefer to say that faith is my response to his initiative.

So far we have seen that faith begins with God. He takes the initiative and I respond. When I respond, a third element comes into being since I have now entered into a relationship with him. Faith (my response) has made that relationship possible. He speaks; I respond, and we begin to get to know each other. And the better I know him, the easier I will find it to respond obediently to him.

All this militates against the idea that faith may be a feeling. Faith may be *accompanied* by feelings. When I tell the primitive Eskimo from the far north that when he punches button 15 he will ride skyward, he may have anything but feelings of inner assurance. Yet when he has gone through the procedure several times, he will experience them. But his feelings will have no bearing on whether he gets to the fifteenth floor or not. Whether he pushes the button tremblingly or with buoyant enthusiasm, the result will be the same. This was why I used Martha as an illustration. The resurrection of Lazarus from the dead did not depend on Martha's feelings of faith but on her overt response to the word of Christ.

But there is more I must say about faith. So far all we have considered is what it means to the person who believes. Before we go on to discuss how we may learn to respond to greater demands of the Word, we must look at the purpose and scope of faith.

THE INVISIBLE AND HOPED FOR

Faith crosses the chasm into the invisible and hoped for.

Hebrews 11:1 is a widely misunderstood verse about faith. In the Revised Standard Version it reads, "Now faith is the assurance of things hoped for, the conviction of things not seen."

At first sight the verse may seem to contradict what I have said about faith not being an inner feeling state. Is it not "assurance"? Is it not "conviction"? Many Bible teachers have in fact taken the verse and used it as a succinct definition of faith, by which we are being taught that faith is a state of being sure or of having a conviction.

To interpret the verse in this way is to ignore its context. The focus of the sentence is elsewhere, and to understand the point the writer is making we must know which words to emphasize.

You can decide for yourself whether I am right or not by studying the passage as a Bible study exercise at the end of this chapter. But for the present, let me italicize those words that in my judgment point to its real focus:

> Now faith is the assurance *of things hoped for*, the conviction *of things not seen*.

The verse addresses itself to the sphere of faith's operation. *Faith is the means by which Christians do business beyond time and space and bring to pass otherwise unrealizable hopes.* Mary's faith made possible the fulfillment of hundreds of years of Jewish longing. It was the means by which the eternal and invisible became mortal and incarnate. Jesus came from beyond outer space through the faith of a peasant girl.

Your own faith then bridges the gap between your humanity and eternity. It can unleash eternal powers here on earth. That is its purpose. You are a bridgehead for the eternal God in the place where he has put you. The whole might of eternity can pass through you to touch people around you. All you do is obey God.

Because obedience is crucial I must return to it. Faith is not given to you in order that you might become a Christian Mr. or Ms. Electric. Although God's awesome power is unleashed when you respond to his Word, faith is not a line to the celestial powerhouse that you may hook up to whatever gadgets you choose.

Faith and obedience are so inseparable as to be one. God gave you faith that you might be one of his agents. Indeed your faith is but one link in a complex chain of circumstances by which God brings his will to pass. Mary's faith was only one of a vast array of factors involved in God's plan to become incarnate. So you are not to be a magician but something infinitely more exciting—a collaborator with the eternal purpose.

INCREASING YOUR FAITH

It may seem that I have been downplaying an emphasis on the amount of faith. And I have. Yet now that we have a clearer understanding of what faith is and of how much can be accomplished with how little, it is time we addressed ourselves to the question of the best way to increase our faith.

But if I have defined faith as the human response to God's initiative, in what terms can I discuss its increase? Either you respond or you don't. Yet the New Testament distinguishes between great faith and little faith. It also talks about *enduring* faith. What do these terms mean?

Strong faith continues to respond to the Word of God in the absence of outward encouragement. It is the faith of my little dog who sits obediently on the lawn when we go shopping and is still waiting for us when we return. It is the church's refusal to abandon the hope of Christ's return. He said he would come soon. That was two thousand years ago.

I grope in my mind for contemporary illustrations of this strong (enduring) faith, but I fail constantly. Each time I think I have one, I find that it is not an example of faith but of a *need* to go on believing. The abandoned wife who refuses to relinquish her belief that her husband will return, the belief of the middle-aged person in the goodness of human political institutions, the patronage of the ballot box in the face of every violation of promise and betrayal of trust—these all exemplify weakness, not strength. They are usually the pathetic defense of vulnerable people to the terrible cutting edge of truth. And that is not what I am talking about.

I am talking about Abraham—old, dried-up Abraham—hobbling to the altar with his manly son and lifting his knife to kill the boy as a sacrifice, believing that the promise made years before would still be fulfilled through this same Isaac, however crazy God's immediate instructions might seem. I am talking about what appears to observers as a smiling insanity, yet what is in fact a glorious gamble with a clear-eyed perception both of what the odds appear to be on the surface and of what they really are. I am talking of Paul singing with Silas in jail at midnight or wind-whipped on the deck of a storm-battered ship, calming the panicky crew with an assurance that all would be well. These all exemplify an irrevocable commitment, not only to principles but to the Word of God—come drought, come tornado, come ten feet of snow. This ability to not quit obeying whatever may seem to go wrong, this is strong faith. To grow in your capacity to persist like this is to increase your faith.

To put it another way, great faith is responding to God *when it is hardest to do so*, either when the thing he demands of you hurts or else seems to be totally impractical.

My earliest experience of the impractical/impossible instruction occurred while I was in the British Navy at the close of World War II. We wanted to advertise our Bible study and prayer meetings in the aircraft carrier on which we were returning from the Far East. I knew I had to approach the skipper—a testy, irascible professional—and do the asking.

"What d'yew want?" he asked as I stood to attention in his cabin. "Hurry. I haven't got time to waste. What? Bible study? I read the lesson on this ship, and we don't need Bible studies."

I stood and waited. There seemed nothing else to do. "Well? What are you waiting for?"

"I want to put up a notice, sir . . ."

"Dammit, didn't you hear what I said? I take Sunday services on this ship. I read the prayers. I read the lesson. Nothing more is needed."

"Yes, sir."

Silence.

"Why are you still standing there, White? The door is behind you."

I felt sick.

"I want to put a notice up, sir . . ."

"Damn you, damn you, *damn you*. Don't I make sense?" (Pause.) "Put your idiotic notice up. Put up any notice you like. Get out!"

"Yes, sir—and thank you very much, sir."

I am not a hero. But *I did* go into the office. And the whole idea seemed crazy. But some men found Christ as a result, and very many were made bolder in their faith.

I'm sorry to go on with theory, but there's something else we must be clear about before we get to "how-tos."

I may have been giving the impression that great faith is rather like great will power. There is a germ of truth in the idea. Faith involves decisions and attitudes, both of which are associated with your volition. But faith is not will power, and will power is not faith. Faith has to do with a personal relationship.

It is faith *in Someone*. When I hang on in the face of what seems like meaninglessness, it is not just self-control I am exercising. Self-control plays very little part. I hang on *because I know who has spoken*. I may have misread what he said, but even that is not terribly important. I know him. I know he is not the kind of person to betray my trust or to let me get beyond his help and care.

Emerson once said that faith is the rejection of a lesser fact and the acceptance of a greater. God is the greater fact. Whatever else impinges on my consciousness, I know he is. I know he cares.

But when you doubt God, you are doubting one of two things about him: his power or his love. Either you doubt he can help you or you doubt that he wants to. To doubt the first is absurd and to doubt the second unthinkable. Yet we do both repeatedly.

How may we stop? How may our faith be increased?

There are several Scripture commands having to do with increased faith. You can increase faith by thinking back on your toughest experiences as a Christian; you may do so by becoming better acquainted with Scripture; you may do so by getting rid of excess spiritual and psychological baggage.

RECALLING BAD TIMES

Have you ever noticed how people who experienced the Great Depression keep harking back to it? They do so with a kind of pride. The effect of the Depression on them was to toughen and strengthen them, and thinking back to the lean years reinforces their resilience.

If you never thought about it, you might expect that positive and beautiful memories would be the ones to increase our faith.

I always believed for instance that one or two really dramatic or miraculous answers to prayer would increase my faith immeasurably. Yet it hasn't worked out that way.

Lorrie (my wife) and I have seen some pretty big miracles in our day. We could, I am sure, collaborate on a "believe-it-or-not" book of incredible answers to prayer. Then why don't we write the book? We don't have time. Such a book is low on our priority list because it would only benefit the bookselling business and our own pockets. It might increase people's faith, but they have a Bible full of better miracles. More to the point, the miracles of which I speak *have not increased our faith at all*. We are ashamed to admit it, but yesterday's miracle does not make today's obedience any easier for us.

The first bit of advice the writer of Hebrews had about increasing faith was to think back to the tough times (Heb 10:32-35). Kenneth Taylor translates the passage as referring to "wonderful days," but see what kind of "wonderful days" they were, even in the *Living Bible*.

> Don't ever forget those wonderful days when you first learned about Christ. Remember how you kept right on with the Lord even though it meant terrible suffering. Sometimes you were laughed at and beaten, and sometimes you watched and sympathized with others suffering the same things. You suffered with those thrown into jail, and you were actually joyful when all you owned was taken from you, knowing that better things were awaiting you in heaven, things that would be yours forever.
>
> Do not let this happy trust in the Lord die away, no matter what happens. Remember your reward!

You would think the writer would have more sense than to remind discouraged Jews of how rough it used to be. After all, it appears from the context that the Jews in question were seriously considering dropping their Christian beliefs. Yet it is precisely to the tough times that he directs their thinking.

Why? I don't altogether know. Tough times, of course, do one of two things to you. They either break or make you. If you are not utterly crushed by them (in which case you will do all you can to bury their memory), you will be enlarged by them. Their pain will make you live more deeply and expand your consciousness. Evidently, the Jews whom the writer addressed had undergone such experiences in their sufferings. God had loomed larger in them. Their experience in Christ proved more exciting. Therefore the memories were pain-wrapped but precious. And when the pain wrappings were taken off and the memories relived, their hearts would be stirred to warm allegiance again. Their faith would be quickened.

If you have only just come to Christ, your rough time may not yet have taken place. But if you've been longer on the way—think back. Remember what happened? How you felt? Doesn't it begin to move you? And aren't you a better person for being stirred in this way? Doesn't a more *solid* sort of faith begin to be rooted?

REMEMBERING THE PROMISES

"Remember your reward!" says the writer of the Hebrew letter (Heb 10:35 LB).

Faith is increased as we acquaint ourselves with Scripture. "Faith cometh . . . by the word of God" (Rom 10:17 KJV). This is underscored by the point in Hebrews 12:1, though most translators and commentators miss the point of what he is saying. "Wherefore seeing we also are compassed about with so great a cloud of witnesses, . . . let us run with patience [or endurance]" (KJV).

What is Scripture saying? Who are the witnesses? Obviously they must be one of two kinds. The witnesses are either *bearing witness to us* or else they are witnesses in the grandstands, that is, *witnesses of us.* "Since we have such a huge crowd of men of faith watching *us from the grandstands* . . ." (Heb 12:1 LB); "With all these *witnesses to faith* around us . . ." (Heb 12:1 NEB).

But the grandstand interpretation of the verse, supported a little by the figure of an athletic event (a race), is not supported by the context as a whole. No, the writer's point is to bring witnesses before us who will testify that *faith is worth it.* Throughout Hebrews 11 he has been telling us of men and women who under the most incredible circumstances endured in their faith. Now he brings the lesson home to us personally by saying that these same people are bearing witness to us. They do not watch from the grandstand. They encourage from the starting line.

Herein lies a very important truth about Scripture. It is the Word of God. But it is in the form of the witness of men and women about God, about his faithfulness, about how he sustains those who trust him. These men and women, through Scripture, bear witness to us about the God of the universe. And their witness is meant to be a source of faith to us.

God could have bypassed the witnesses. He could have dictated to someone in a trance. But he chose, in the main, to give his infallible Word through the experiences and words of fallible men and women.

In this way the Bible is doubly personal. It is personal in that it is a personal message from God to each one of us. We must study it if we want more faith. But it is also personal in the sense that it is a message from flesh-and-blood men and women across the centuries to us. By the Spirit these people gather round us as we prepare ourselves for the race of faith.

Therefore you must study Scripture in order to grow in faith. Study the lives of bygone heroes of faith. Discover how human they were and how slow to learn. Modern biographies of outstanding Christians might depress you, whereas the scriptural narrative of the life of Abraham or David will enable you to discover how patient God is in training essentially feeble believers to make them giants of faith.

As you study Scripture other changes will take place in you too. The promises of God will sometimes come home to you with peculiar power and sweetness. They will be of enormous help to you as you try to be obedient at times of difficulty. Again, your study will throw light on problems that impeded your faith. The Holy Spirit will clear up at least some of the problems that bothered you as you become better acquainted with the Word of God.

The Christ of the Scriptures will also be food on which your faith will grow. A vision of his strength and power will uplift you, for you will begin to discover that the same strength and power are available for you. His endurance in the face of opposition will not only inspire you. You will see it as an endurance he wants to share with you so that it becomes yours.

How would the young pianist feel if just before a recital Arthur Rubinstein grabbed his or her elbow and said, "I know how it feels. I've had some pretty bad times before critical audiences. But stick with it. It's worth it. I'll be rooting for you." Such a young pianist would sit not on a piano stool but on a cushion of air to play explosions of light and caresses of angels.

And this is your lot. Moses is at your elbow as you approach the starting point. So are Joshua and Rahab. So too are thousands of unknowns who went through hell on earth and proved God true. They are straining to speak to you, to tell you something and about someone.

GETTING RID OF EXCESS BAGGAGE

But it's a race all right, a race of faith, a long and grueling race in which you cannot afford to be weighed down. Unconfessed sin and useless priorities will weaken your faith. It is easy enough to understand why unconfessed sin will impede faith. I won't go into the matter at this point. But what about the useless priorities?

A Christian is a one-priority person. Jesus made it clear what his followers had to be. "Ye cannot serve God and mammon," he stated bluntly (Mt 6:24 KJV). A Christian cannot have a vivid faith when torn in two directions at once.

It is precisely here that many Christians fail. Attracted by money, pleasure, career, position or prestige, they try to close their eyes to the fact that human nature makes it impossible for us to have more than one supreme goal in life. Ask them what their supreme goal is and they'll say, "To glorify God, to serve Christ," and so on. But watch their lives and you'll be puzzled. Talk to them and you'll find a strange lack of excitement about the glory of God. You'll also find little evidence of vital faith.

Most of my Christian physician colleagues are doctors first and Christians second. They would be reluctant to admit this and might accuse me of being judgmental. Nevertheless it is a fact, a fact not peculiar to physicians but also true of Christian lawyers, teachers and others. But no one can serve two masters: "He will either hate the first and love the second, or treat the first with respect and the second with scorn" (Mt 6:24 JB).

If I think of myself as a psychiatrist who is also a Christian, I'm in trouble. When I think of myself as a Christian who also practices psychiatry, I am not only more free to serve Christ, I do a better job at psychiatry. The distinction is not subtle but fundamental. It has to do with goals and loyalties, prime goals and prime loyalties, and with the nature of freedom and slavery.

The unnecessary weight does not have to be a career goal, however. It can be almost anything—trivial or important. Christian mother, what are you—Christ's follower who is also called to do a good job of mothering, or a mother who is also a Christian? When Satan comes to you and says, "Back off on your Christian stand, and I will not hurt your child," what do you do?

Christ calls us inflexibly and uncompromisingly to one loyalty. Unless you can identify and ditch competing goals and loyalties, you will never be a man or woman of faith.

BEING TRIED BY FIRE

So far we have talked of what *you* can do to increase your faith. To some extent we have ignored what God is doing and how you may cooperate with him.

The goal of increasing your faith is his goal even more than it is yours. He has been working actively on it since before you became a Christian in ways which, given the preference, you would hardly have chosen for yourself.

As fire refines gold, so "when the heat is on" your dross will surface, and twenty-four-carat faith gradually develops underneath (1 Pet 1:7). As drought drives the roots of trees deeper underground, so your faith will send roots downward into the ground of your being in times that seem spiritually dry. And you will be green in drought.

Both fire and drought are part of God's disciplinary process. He trains, disciplines, shapes you as a runner in the race of faith, as a fighter in the warfare of faith. The training involves correction and pain. Your faith will increase or decrease according to how you respond to his intervention.

Hebrews 10:32—12:13 ends by discussing faith as a personal relationship in a family (Heb 12:5-11). Faith grows by painful discipline carried out by the father of the family.

A child is not a programmable computer. Different children will respond differently to the same discipline. The child chooses. He or she cooperates with the process or sabotages it. The writer to the Hebrews knows this. He points it out to the Jews who are wavering between belief and unbelief. The Christian Jews can choose what they do about the discipline. God is not a Celestial Programmer.

But in facing their choice they must keep a number of things in mind. First, discipline is an evidence of parental love. To receive no discipline means you are a "love child" rather than a loved child. "When he whips you it proves you are really his child" (Heb 12:6 LB).

Again they must realize that discipline is painful. It is not "punishment." Punishment is retributive. Discipline is purposeful training. "Discipline . . . is never pleasant; at the time it seems painful" (Heb 12:11 NEB). Criticism from the trainer, grueling hours of extra exercise, sweat, weariness and pain are all part of the deal for the athlete. Should Christian training in the exercise of faith be any less rigorous?

But the crunch lies in how the Christian responds to the discipline. It is this that determines whether faith will blossom or wither.

Years ago when plastic surgery was less developed than it now is, patients often underwent painful operations to improve their appearance. Some surgeons felt that anesthetics, whether local or general, would interfere with the final result. Carol Lombard, after a car accident, was said to have been faced with the choice of severe pain on the operating table or the loss of her beauty. She chose pain.

But the pain itself did not regain her loveliness for her. Two elements combined to do this: the surgeon's skill and Miss Lombard's stillness. Had she been unwilling during the operation to endure pain quietly, had she struggled or twisted her head as the scalpel was cutting or the needle suturing, then the same operation that restored beauty could have produced a disastrous deformity.

"Discipline, no doubt, is never pleasant; at the time it seems painful, but in the end it yields for those who have been trained by it the peaceful harvest of an honest life" (Heb 12:11 NEB).

For those who have been trained by it. Here is the crux of the matter. You may have the beauty of God's image restored in you by corrective soul surgery. God's tenderness and skill are at your disposal. The knife is poised; the sutures ready. How will you respond? Will you wriggle and squirm? Or will you quietly thank him, not for the pain but for the process of correction associated with it?

God does not change you by magic. No wand will be waved over your head so that your deepest problems vanish overnight. There may be breakthroughs, sudden insights, glorious experiences. But the major work of transformation will be slow and often deeply painful. Yet the pain is immeasurably reduced by trust and understanding.

When my oldest boy, Scott, had his first bad fall as a toddler, he split his chin widely with a gash that extended up into the floor of his mouth. At that time we were far from civilization in Bolivia. I had no surgical instruments, only a pair of eyebrow tweezers and household needles and thread. I had no means of relieving pain. Firm hands gripped his tiny form as I inflicted what must have seemed like unbelievable pain on my terrified son. To say my heart was breaking sounds sentimental, yet his pain was my pain. There's no way I could comfort him with the knowledge that all would be well. Why did I have to frighten as well as hurt him? I agonized over his ordeal as I gripped his tender skin with eyebrow tweezers and brutally jabbed a sewing needle again and again into his chin.

But I learned two things. First, that God is not a sadist. He takes no pleasure in our pain. If I, a human father, agonized so deeply over the pain I was inflicting on my child, how much more did my heavenly Father grieve over our sorrows? Isaiah taught this as fact hundreds of years ago. "In all their affliction, he [God] was afflicted" (Is 63:9 ASV).

I also discovered that although pain is magnified by fear, it is dramatically alleviated by understanding and trust. I could not convey what I was doing to Scott, but God can and does convey it to us. I have found that in the midst of the psychological stresses and pains of certain experiences, if only I understood or even trusted, the pain was turned into joy. Trusting, I became a collaborator with God in the operations by which he remade his image in me and deepened my faith.

"Count it all joy," writes James, "when ye fall into divers temptations [that is, trials]; knowing this, that the trying of your faith worketh patience [that is, endurance]" (Jas 1:2-3 KJV). It is in this sense that we rejoice in sufferings. We do not do so because suffering is good but because God uses suffering, even when it arises from sin, as an instrument to perfect our faith and to make it tough and enduring. It is possible then not only to have our faith immeasurably increased according to the way we respond to trials but to discover that the pain of the trials can be transmuted into joy. Therefore you must thank God in the midst of your pain. Tell him you trust him. Praise him for what he can do, for what he is doing. As you do so pressures will lift. You will be given a garment of praise to replace a spirit of heaviness.

These and other lessons about how my faith could be perfected came home to me climactically one day in Bolivia. Oppressed by what I felt was far more than my share of trials, and feeling myself bereft of human comfort and understanding, I cried to God one Saturday afternoon to give me "just one word of comfort." I asked for a crumb, and in the end he gave me a banquet.

Because of the pressures, I decided to take the next day (Sunday) off. Lorrie and I would not even attend morning service but would cross the river behind the tiny Bolivian settlement of Tambo and climb through the semidesert to the top of a steep hill overlooking the river valley.

Some of the pressures slipped away temporarily almost as soon as we had forded the river. God ministers peace through nature. With the sun warming our bodies we climbed between thorny shrubs, giant cactus and kapok trees, helping each other over the steep places and clambering determinedly upward. The settlement below began to appear like a beautiful toy world. An intense blueness in the sky colored the foam-flecked river below.

Half way up the hill we stopped to rest and to hold our own mini-worship service. We had a Gideon New Testament, and as we sat together we turned to the back of it where one or two hymns were printed. With no particular thought in mind we selected a hymn and began to sing.

How firm a foundation, ye saints of the Lord,
Is laid for your faith in His excellent word!
What more can He say than to you He hath said,
To you who for refuge to Jesus have fled?

What more can He say than to you He hath said? A bomb went off in my skull. I had been asking for a word and here was God saying that he had already said all that needed saying. I began to cry—for joy and relief. Faith cometh by the Word of God.

Lorrie went on singing.

When through fiery trials thy pathway shall lie,
My grace, all sufficient, shall be thy supply;
The flame shall not hurt thee; I only design
Thy dross to consume, and thy gold to refine.

So suffering did have meaning. God was doing something through my trial.

When through the deep waters I cause thee to go,
The rivers of sorrow shall not overflow;
For I will be with thee, thy trial to bless,
And sanctify to thee thy deepest distress.

I will be with thee, thy trial to bless. It was not a cold inhuman process. The warm breath of Aslan was about me and the fragrance of his mane.

> The soul that on Jesus hath leaned for repose,
> I will not, I will not desert to its foes;
> That soul, though all hell should endeavor to shake,
> I'll never, no never, no never forsake.[1]

I am unclear as to what happened next. I know my nose was running and that Lorrie was being very motherly. But nothing mattered. A radiance far greater than that of the mountain air had broken over me, and I felt the strength of ten men. Soon we were climbing upward again, struggling happily against the downward pull of gravity and the vicious stabs of cactus and thorn bushes.

And in a sense we've been climbing ever since—gravity and thorns notwithstanding.

A PASSAGE TO STUDY

Read Hebrews 10:32—12:13.

1. Hebrews 10:32-39. Enduring faith may be helped by calling to mind past trials (vv. 32-34). But what evidences are there in these verses that having faith or not having it is something that is placed under my control?

2. Hebrews 11. Pick out those examples in this chapter that have to do with the "not seen" and the "hoped for," and try to show how the writer illustrates his thesis in verse 1 by the examples that follow.

3. Hebrews 12:1-13. In what way does "looking to Jesus" help our faith? What response are we to make in the midst of disciplinary pain? Are you making that response?

7

Changed Relationships

———— ❧ ————

As a Christian you are a person with two families: heavenly and earthly. In becoming a Christian you began your relationship with the first and changed your relationships in the second. The course of relationships in both rarely remains untroubled. No fights are so fierce as Christian fights, and no quarrels so bitter as family quarrels. On the other hand no fellowship can be so warm as Christian fellowship, and no shelter so comforting as a home where relationships are what they should be. It is important then that we look at both families carefully.

THE BIOLOGICAL FAMILY

I was once asked to give a seminar on "A Whole Family in a Fragmented World." The seminar was for Christians, many of whom must have assumed that Christianity would knit fragmented families together. And so it may. But equally well, it may create new tensions and clashing loyalties. "Think not that I am come to send peace on earth: I came not to send peace, but a sword," Jesus asserted. "For I came to set a man at variance against his father. . . . And a man's foes shall be they of his own household" (Mt 10:34-36 KJV).

Social workers, marriage counselors and family therapists proclaim the importance of the family unit. It is true that voices are raised predicting the doom of the family. But they are lone voices, scarcely heard among the general clamor. There may be different theories about *how* families function, but there is almost unanimous opinion that function they must.

As important as the family is, there are yet more important things. If unity in the family can only exist at the expense of its members' loyalty to Jesus Christ, then the good has become the enemy of the best. You must be loyal to Christ whatever it may cost you *or anyone close to you*. There must be no compromise.

It would be wrong to suggest that Christ's aim is to stir up a hornet's nest in your home. God creates institutions to work—not to fall apart. The family is one of *his* institutions. But sometimes a structure has been so undermined that it needs to be pulled apart and rebuilt before it can stand. Therefore an explosion in a family, however painful it may be, need not dismay you. It may result from a sickness that has been there for years. Or it may represent a clearing of debris that presages a new building.

There may be difficulty when you let your family know about your relationship with Christ. Tensions may increase if you are loyal to your new Master. But be clear about one thing: tensions may increase, but it must never be your aim to increase them. Anger may come, but you must never seek to stir it up. Making and breaking families is God's business, not yours.

In no place must you watch your attitude more carefully than in your own family. Christians tend to be a little self-righteous at home, new Christians especially so. Beware of "righteous indignation" about the sins of other family members. Show others the same mercy and patience that Christ showed you. Do you feel that your family has had all the mercy it deserves? Well, so had you, long before God got through to you.

Here is a word both of caution and of reassurance: of *reassurance*, because any feeling of hesitation you have about telling your family about Christ is understandable; of *caution*, first, because however kindly and tactfully you confess your allegiance to Christ, the news may be received coldly or even lead to alienation, and second, because you must beware of becoming the family prig.

Things may turn out well. You may find the whole family prepared by the Holy Spirit and hungry for truth. This happens. The whole family may turn to Christ and believe. More commonly, however, the immediate results are less pleasing. The acceptance of your confession will most likely differ from one family member to another.

New constellations of intrafamily alliances may make their appearances, and you must be on the watch for them. It is not your job to line up supporters for the Christian cause. Your job is to be a center of truth, love and light in your home. This does not require you to be unnatural. Be yourself in your family, but let that self belong to God.

THE FAMILY: A SCRIPT TO FOLLOW, A SCORE TO DANCE

The family remains at its healthiest only when its members relate as God designed them to relate. Social change may modify its size or its links with the rest of the world, but nothing has and nothing ever will alter its essential nature.

God designed humans to live in families. God is not a bachelor; he is a Trinity. God comes to us not just as Father but as a Three-in-One; and humans, created in his image, are created also with an innate capacity for intimate personal relationships. The family unit arises out of what God is in the very core of his being.

The God who created humanity made the basics of family relationships explicit. To be God's servant in your family involves living out your special role (child, parent or whatever) as it is conceived in the inspired script. There is no more powerful way than this of bearing witness to your family or of being God's agent of change and healing there. And remember, your role does not include that of general judge and critic.

Long before I ever became a psychiatrist, I found myself involved in what is now known as family counseling. Because I was familiar with the biblical script for family role-playing, I would frequently point out to a father, a husband or a wife exactly what the script called for. Very soon I became accustomed to a stock reaction, which in summary ran something like this: "Yes, I know the Bible says I ought to love my wife, but it also says she should obey me. And she doesn't. I'll start playing my part when she starts playing hers."

I call this the "Yes . . . but" response, and with slight word changes it can be placed in the mouth of any family member. In essence it pleads that we can't be expected to fulfill our role in the family properly unless every other member of the family is fulfilling theirs.

I hesitate to dismiss the protest out of hand. Yet you can see at once that it forms an impossible basis for family living. If each family member must first make sure about the satisfactory role-playing of all other family members, or even of any one of them, the home becomes a forum for endless bickering. Each member's commitment to the unit becomes tentative and fragile. No stability is possible. But the essence of family relationships is that they be, like God's relationship with us, based on unswerving commitment. It is the solid unconditional commitment of family members to one another that makes the growth of rich personal relations possible.

This then must form the foundation stone of your relationship to your family. There must be a solid, unswerving commitment to God to play whatever your role may be in the family for his sake and without any regard to how well other family members play theirs. This is part of your Christian commitment. The others may reject you. The family as a whole may turn you out. But until it does, you are committed to God's script for father, son, wife, mother, husband or whatever. Even if the family throws you out, you should be ready at the drop of a hat to resume your role.

Each role is played in relation to other roles. Or, to change the image from a play to a ballet, you do not pirouette in isolation. In the conjugal pas de deux, while there must be submission by each dancer to the other, the principal steps for the husband are those of love and sacrifice while those of the wife are of submission and reverence (Eph 5:21-33). The steps must be rehearsed constantly if a beautiful performance is to take place.

Much of the unpopularity of the score arises because we bring our rigid and barren modern thinking to bear on it. We confuse equality with sameness, and while apparently asking for the one, in reality we are asking for the other. The result is not a pas de deux but a nondance—drab, gray and unsatisfying.

Or else the dancing is competitive, each in the conjugal dance vying to take over the more desirable steps from the other. Understandably, the partners frequently come to grief—now tangling and tripping ungracefully, now soaring to crash from empty space where welcoming arms should have been.

God does not make the husband responsible for the wife's submission or the wife responsible for the husband's love. Each is to follow the score that is written for him or her. Therefore leave God with the responsibility of dealing with your partner's failure. Concentrate on your own steps.

You might ask, "Isn't the whole business a masochistic exercise in futility?" Even if it were, we should still dance by the score. Yet to do so is not masochistic, for often it is an experience in joy, not in pain. And as for being futile, it can produce powerful effects. We may not be trained dancers, but we can be compared with them in that there is something deep within a family relationship that is analogous to the feeling of a dancer who responds to a another dancer performing his or her part perfectly. There is a stirring within our limbs to respond to the perfection and beauty of what we see and to be drawn into the dance for sheer wonder. Bitterness and rebellion slowly melt away and our feet come to life. Therefore when you dance with skill and vigorous abandon, I begin to feel an inner pull. It may take you some time to get my feet tapping, but I cannot deny the urge that is within me (1 Pet 3:1-2).

Yet whether other feet are stirred to dance or not, the choreographer has written a score for you. Dance it. Your temptation will be to indulge in fantasies about the kind of family you would like to have around you. Such fantasies may be turned into prayer, and it could be that much of the frustration in your family life springs from the fact that you have one program that you are striving for while God has another. *It is not God's prime aim to make your family nice for you to live with.* He may even want you to learn lessons about making things easier on them. Or his plans may encompass things you never dreamed of.

I cannot promise that your family tragedies, like those of the biblical patriarch Jacob's, will prove to be the salvation of Western civilization, but I do know God has plans that are wider than your family unit. I also know he brings good out of evil and that he cares about your frustrations and hurts. Don't cling rigidly therefore to any set plan of your own about the family's future. Leave the future with God and trust him.

THE FAMILY OF GOD

You are a member of the family of God. You were cleansed by the same blood, regenerated by the same Spirit. You are a citizen of the same city, a slave of the same Master, a reader of the same Scriptures, a worshiper of the same God. The same presence dwells silently in you as in them.

Therefore you are committed to them and they to you. They are your brothers, sisters, fathers, mothers and children in God. Whether you like or dislike them, you belong to them. You have responsibilities toward them that must be discharged in love. As long as you live on this earth, you are in their debt. Whether they have done much or little for you, Christ has done all. He demands that your indebtedness to him be transferred to your new family.

We are not allowed to choose our brothers and sisters or

whether we will be committed to them or not. They belong to us and we to them. We have no control over the fact that we are to love, care and be responsible for them. We may fail to live up to our commitment and rebel against Christ. But our rebellion does not abolish the commitment. It will be there as long as life endures.

You are committed to *all* your new brothers and sisters. With some you will discover an instant affinity. There will be a spontaneous warmth and a pleasure in their company. But others will repel you. You will find yourself avoiding them, being irritated by them or else having no feelings at all about them except boredom. But you are not to confine yourself to the favorite few.

It is better so. Where commitment is based on attraction, it is as temporary as the attraction. It is not, in fact, commitment at all. A relationship bound together by mutual attraction will prove an unstable relationship. More to the point, the parties to such a relationship are compelled to work at being attractive. The moment they fail to be attractive enough, they may alienate the people who matter to them. Far from being a haven in which to take refuge, then, relationships based on attraction become a source of anxiety and strain.

So you can see at once that there must be better ways of making people work at their relationships. If I am kind to you only because I want you to go on liking me, then my kindness is phony. We need real kindness to surround us, not commercial or neurotic kindness. We need lovingkindness based on commitment.

You need it yourself. Somewhere in this world you need a body of people who will always accept you and always care for you whether you are attractive or not. If you sin, they may rebuke you. They may demand that you repent or put something right. But they will never disown you, never abandon you and never stop caring. Their commitment to you is not based on their admiration for you but on the more solid ground of Christ's person and work.

So when Christ demands you commit yourself to an enduring responsibility toward people you may not naturally care for, he is really doing you a favor. He is insisting that you facilitate the very thing you need, a caring community whose members never fail one another.

But where, you may ask, is such a community to be found?

It already exists, and you are a part of it. It is not as though God asks you to start from scratch and build such a community from nothing. There already is a community of saints, bound together by blood, water, spiritual life and the power of God. The fact that its members sometimes fail to live up to their commitment does not destroy the community. It is there. It will not go away. And your relationship with it is something God takes with utter seriousness.

FINDING A CHURCH HOME

So far I have only stated the matter in general terms, but now I must be practical. How can your responsibility to God's people be worked out from day to day? Take church membership for instance. Let me mention some down-to-earth principles.

If you do not already belong to a church, try to find one where God's Word is honored and taught clearly and helpfully. It is my personal conviction that the denomination matters less than the health of the local congregation. Ask advice from Christian friends you trust. Pray about the matter. When you select a church, attend it for several weeks and try to get to know people there. Make a point of introducing yourself to the pastor.

Don't be in a hurry to join until you are sure you are making the right decision. On the other hand don't expect the church to be free of faults and inconsistencies. Few are. If you are looking for the ideal church, you will look for a long time.

Remember that if the people who attend the church belong to Christ, they are your brothers and sisters. The presence of God the Holy Spirit is in their midst. Some members may have irritating peculiarities. Yet who are you to take offense when Christ has received them? In joining a local congregation you are joining a group of sinners on whom God has had mercy, just as he had mercy on you. The church is not a country club.

If you should already be a member of a church, think about the matter long and hard before changing. Perhaps you have recently come to Christ. If so it is understandable that you should view your church through different eyes. If you belong to a church where Christian conversions take place regularly and where provision is made to help those who are embarking on a new life, there will be no problem. On the other hand you may get the feeling that in your church people will not understand and may not even approve your newfound joy.

Beware of sudden moves. You may find, as you listen with awakened ears and watch with enlightened eyes, that there were things going on in your local church that you had never been aware of. You may find others who share your experience of Christ or that the pastor is longing for someone like you to come along. Therefore pray that God will enable you to find any true Christian fellowship that may be available in the church.

Don't become either an instant pharisee or set yourself up to be martyred and misunderstood. Pray that God will give you an appropriate opportunity to share your new faith with someone in the church. Ask the minister for half an hour of his time and explain to him or her as clearly as you can what has happened to you. Should you find yourself treated defensively or in an amused patronizing manner, don't rush off in a huff. God will show you, in time, what he wants you to do.

In any event, make sure you find some group of Christians inside or outside the church with whom you can pray and study the Scriptures. Meet regularly with them. Try to look on the weekly experience not as an *activity* you have joined but as *a body of people* to whom you belong. A small fellowship, prayer and Bible study group cannot be stressed enough. Whatever else you have to cut out, don't cut this. You were meant to grow and develop spiritually as part of a body and in fellowship with others.

On the other hand I want to stress with equal force the need for you to belong to a church.

Christ died that humans of every type be reconciled to God and to one another. The genius of Christianity is that it makes possible ongoing fellowship between people who could not otherwise tolerate, let alone enjoy, one another. Christ gets refined socialites hobnobbing with migrant farm workers; middle-aged squares weeping with rebels and swingers; blacks, Indians, Jews and WASPs praying earnestly together; and management and labor sharing each other's problems. Christ alone can make incompatibles mesh.

TOO MANY MEETINGS

You can attend too many meetings. Christian students often excuse neglected studies on the grounds that they were "doing the

Lord's work." Husbands and wives neglect their families for the same reason. Important as meetings are, you can misuse them. They can serve as an escape from less congenial duties. And tragically, where Christian gatherings serve as an escape, they lose their spiritual value. God wishes us to confront reality, not to escape from it.

God does not gauge spirituality by the number of meetings you attend or how much time you devote to a Christian friend. He is more concerned with the spirit in which you tackle each duty. Therefore think carefully about how much time you spend in "Christian" activities. Make sure you never use them as an escape from less congenial duties. As a Christian you are to give *all* you do, everything you've got.

THE WE-THEY DICHOTOMY

Considering all the divisions that have plagued Christianity for two thousand years, it is amazing that God has continued to use the church to extend his kingdom. To this day covert battles are raging, hostilities and suspicions fermenting and breeding. Loudly touted church unions patch outward differences while discontent and bitterness seethe within. And for every amalgamation in one place there will be a couple of breakups some place else.

What can you do about it?

The first thing you must not do is to let the situation throw you. Christ is still in control and he knows what he is doing. His plans are ripening. No sinful strife evades his watchful eyes. What may cause you to be appalled and deeply discouraged may grieve but never dismay him. Nothing can or will slow down his forward thrust to final victory and judgment. One day he will root up and fling away many fences that divide his people. Therefore adopt his perspective. Raise your head above dismaying pettiness of local strife and share his victorious stance. As a follower of Christ you cannot afford to grow cynical and disillusioned.

Big hassles. The next thing is to decide what responsibility you have for the situations you know about. They are of two kinds, which may overlap but can be referred to as big hassles and small hassles. When I talk about big hassles, I am referring not to the heat or fierceness of the divisions but to the number of people involved. Big hassles involve whole churches, whole denominations or Christian organizations.

So often I have been among evangelical groups who are obsessed with what I will call the "we-they" dichotomy. *They* refer to the members of another Christian group. *They* are always the same; they can be predicted to act in a certain way, to say certain things, to hold identical views and to share identical errors. *Their* characters are remarkably similar. *We*, on the other hand, in addition to being right, all have different characters. Some of us are more spiritual than others; we tend to have different strong points. We complement one another's strengths and weaknesses. *We* are human. *They*, in contrast, are stereotypes.

We tend to view Christians and non-Christians alike not as they really are but through prejudicial filters that distort their images. It may be that we are afraid. Truth is very important. Our grasp of it is feeble. It bolsters our courage to protect ourselves from being intellectually or spiritually ravished. So we dehumanize and stereotype *them* in our minds in order to render them less threatening and ourselves less vulnerable.

There is nothing wrong about knowing you are right. By all

means hold on to the truth firmly. Indeed, you need never be afraid that anyone will take it away from you. The truth is a Person. He will never leave or forsake you. Therefore be zealous to proclaim it and him.

You may have little occasion to meet people of other organizations and traditions. In any case, they too may share the fearful tendency to view the world through we-they spectacles, and may view *you* as threatening, deceived and dangerous. But don't play the same game. Remember that people on the other side of a religious fence are still people. They may even be Christians. So have a courteous and respectful attitude toward them. Remember they have hopes, problems and fears just as you do. Share anything about Christ that you can without trying to lure them over the dividing fence. Then leave to Christ the matter of the hassle that raised the fence for which neither you nor your acquaintance is responsible.

Small hassles. But it is the small hassles, not the big ones, that will render you a casualty in the warfare against the powers of hate: the hassles inside the local church or the fellowship groups you belong to. You find yourself irritated by the smugness and patronizing attitude of brother Smith. You feel vaguely guilty about your critical feelings, but then Mr. Smith is smug and is patronizing. Are you supposed to wear blinders? Again, Miss Kalansky has been criticizing you behind your back. You resent her. What are you supposed to do? Forgive her? Talk to her?

Let's say your fellowship group is divided on a doctrinal issue. Feelings are running high. Your doctrinal views are with one party, yet you sense that the whole matter has less to do with doctrine than with bruised egos. What should you do?

I would prefer not to discuss how to cope with hassles but

how to take a positive approach. Ask: How may we promote unity among God's people? Earlier I mentioned the importance of commitment and closeness among Christians of widely differing backgrounds. Yet I said little about how such closeness may be achieved in practice or about the dangers of seeking fellowship as an end in itself.

THE HEART OF CHRISTIAN FELLOWSHIP

There is more to Christian fellowship than commitment, human closeness or even heterogeneity. You can get a wonderful feeling of being accepted for your naked self from therapy groups and encounter groups. You can experience esprit de corps and comradeship in a wartime military unit. The experience of "fellowship" can be intense, uplifting and humbling even though it is not Christian.

What is it, then, that distinguishes Christian fellowship from every other form of closeness, oneness, togetherness or whatever? Why is it so important that its uniqueness be experienced when so many psychological substitutes are available? What makes truly Christian fellowship so difficult yet so vital to achieve?

For many Christian writers the heart of the matter lies in the Greek word *koinonia*. Koinonia is a New Testament word that has to do with sharing something. The something you share may be a material object, like a fishing boat, or an experience of Christ. A sort of mystique has developed around the word, almost as though pronouncing it or understanding its etymology produces Christian fellowship. But you can talk koinonia till the cows come home and never discover what Christian fellowship is about.

The capacity to experience fellowship (to share, to be close, to know) was given by God to all people but was mutilated by sin. Sin has damaged our capacity to know one another because it damaged our capacity to know God. Therefore any attempt to mend the broken fragments of humanity, however exciting or apparently successful, will be illusory and doomed to ultimate failure unless humanity's relationship with God is restored.

I can't have true fellowship with you unless both of us have fellowship with God. I can love you, feel close to you, enjoy your emotional support. But sooner or later the thing will go sour or remain too shallow to satisfy. Unless both of us experience the healing and reconciling of God through Christ, unless both of us are restored to an ever-deepening relationship with God, then anything we have going between us will be a mere echo of the real thing.

The heart of the matter does not lie in *sharing* (koinonia). If sharing were the crucial point, it really would not matter too much *what* we shared. The relationships arising from whatever was shared would be comparable.

But the results are not comparable. At the heart of Christian fellowship is reconciliation, the restoration of your relationship to God. For you can only truly know someone else through God and in God. All other knowing is at least partially illusory.

And your relationship with God is an ongoing thing. It involves what John calls "walking in light" (1 Jn 1:3-7), that is, maintaining that restored relationship with God by allowing the Holy Spirit to point out your sin and failure, and responding accordingly. As the miracle of the eternal reconciliation is daily renewed in your experience, so too your capacity to have Christian fellowship with another brother or sister will be enhanced.

Here then is the heart of Christian fellowship. It does not have to do primarily with our relationship with one another but rather with our common relationship to God. It is only *in him* that we are one. It is only by making our relationship *with him* primary that our relationships with one another will be what they should be. We cannot be reconciled to another unless we are reconciled to him. Nor can we truly be reconciled to him unless we also be reconciled to one another.

MAKING IT WORK

True Christian fellowship, then, will be an outworking of a restored relationship with God. It will arise naturally and spontaneously where my relationship with God is healthy. On the other hand, where you and I fail to experience fellowship, our failure will serve as a sensitive barometer indicating that one or both of us have an impaired relationship with God.

But the fact that we fail to get along does not necessarily mean that individually we should fly to our secret chamber and spend an hour in prayer. There is often no call to pray; the solution may be plain if both of us will only see it. If, for instance, it is my duty to forgive you, there is no need to pray for guidance. I must forgive. That is all there is to it. Even to pray for strength to forgive may be a subtle way of postponing forgiveness.

The rules for maintaining Christian fellowship are simple but tough. You will find them in several parts of the New Testament. For example, "Let nothing be done through strife or vainglory" (Phil 2:3-4 KJV).

What motivates you in the activities of your Christian group? How much of it is either competitive or an attempt to win approval?

Strife. In context the word implies the wish to insist on your way because you resent someone else. Your proposed action may be right in itself. But what makes you push it so hard? Does Joe get under your skin, and do you sense that he will oppose it? Or do you pursue the matter because of Mary's tendency to steamroller her wishes over everyone else's?

Let nothing be done through strife. Joe's and Mary's ideas may be wrong, and their spirit inappropriate. But fighting them with their own weapons destroys fellowship. You mustn't fight them at all. The real enemy is the sower of discord, and to fight him you begin by putting right your feelings toward Joe and Mary. Having done so, you ask God whether you are really right about what you thought God wanted. If you are, God may require that you stand firm on your ideas. But standing firm must never be due to your feelings toward Joe or Mary.

The problem of coming to grips with your feelings about Joe and Mary is that it will involve pain for you. To sacrifice resentment is to murder your darling child. It becomes easier when you recognize that Joe and Mary have their own hang-ups and insecurities that call for compassion rather than resentment. It also helps to realize that God cares tenderly for Joe and Mary in spite of what you see as their undesirable qualities.

Therefore lay your resentful feelings on the altar and offer them up in praise to God. Whenever you catch yourself indulging in fantasies of triumphing over Mary or putting Joe in his place, bind your fantasies to the same altar and give them the same treatment. Ruthlessly. Promptly. Always.

Stick with your point if you're sure of it but without riding it to death. If other people buy Joe's and Mary's schemes, don't sulk. God can afford to wait. Be a cheerful dissenter and someone who disagrees courteously and charitably.

Let nothing be done through strife or *vainglory*. You must do nothing in the group with the idea of exciting admiration. Have you discovered a contribution you can make? Something you excel at? Have praises been whispered in your ear? Is there someone else who is not as competent as you? *Let nothing be done through vainglory*. It kills fellowship.

"Do nothing from selfishness or conceit, but in humility count others better than yourselves" (Phil 2:3). So there's something you're good at. Of course you recognize you have your weaknesses. In fact sometimes you feel low. But you're not the lowest person on the totem pole. Would you say you're around the halfway mark? Or higher?

Paul poses an intellectual problem. How can most of us "count others better" than ourselves? Can we do so and remain intellectually honest? After all, we can't all be the *most* inferior. That unhappy position belongs to only one of us. The rest of us range somewhere between the best and the worst. Would it not be more honest to assess yourself realistically in terms of your place in the scale of values?

By all means be realistic, but what are you measuring when you assess your worth over against Cynthia's? Your scholastic achievement? Your athletic ability? Your appearance? Your personality? Your enthusiasm about Christian things? Your years of experience? Some aggregate of all of these?

For which one of these can you take any personal credit? If they are God-given things, they do not make you *better* than Cynthia, only *more fortunate*. They should be a cause of humble gratitude. And if you have been diligent and think you can take credit for something, it may be worth less than you think. Human efforts rate low in the divine scale of values.

Paul's position is an existential rather than an intellectual one. In discovering the gifts and virtues of others, he has been awed and overwhelmed. He realizes that the question of who is the better person is complex. But in any case it is irrelevant to him. He is more impressed by the gifts of others than by his own.

My father-in-law is a Nova Scotian fisherman. He lacks my years of university training. I could talk more impressively than he on world events, philosophy, the limitations of the scientific method and on and on. But let us put out to sea in a boat off the rocky coast of Cape Breton. He seems by instinct to know the depth of the water everywhere. In an uncanny way he can find any port within two hundred miles in a fog without navigational aids. I become a stupid landlubber, helplessly inept and outclassed by this sea-taught marvel of a man.

Moreover when he visits my home he wanders around noting what needs to be fixed. I am clumsy with tools, bewildered in the face of practical jobs. He fixes my lopsided garden gate. What to me was a formidable difficulty is to him an afternoon's recreation.

Am I a better man than he? By what scale are the two of us to be measured? Who can say which of us is *morally* superior? Through my own prayers and ministry he recently came back to God after years of wandering. Yet now his joy in Christ and in the Scriptures makes me ashamed. He seems to have progressed more in a few months than I in years. With none of the Bible training or helpful influences to which I have been subjected, he has come far. I stand rebuked before him.

Who will assess us and tell us which of us is the better man before God?

Do you have problems holding other Christians to be better than yourself? If so, pray that God will reveal his greatness and his grace to you. Wait in his presence saying, "My soul, wait thou only upon God." Continue the practice for months—for the rest of your life if need be. And as you see him and see yourself before him, you will have no problem esteeming others better than yourself. You won't crawl. You won't even feel inferior. You will just rejoice in God—and in the wonder of what he is doing in people around you. And in thus rejoicing you will fulfill a basic condition of Christian fellowship.

"Let each of you look not only to his own interests, but also to the interests of others" (Phil 2:4). I pass through deep waters emotionally. Suddenly in the midst of my trouble God breaks through. A new insight turns my darkness to day, my groaning to joy. In the fellowship meeting I share what has happened with my brothers and sisters who praise God with me for it. But Bill seizes the opportunity to tell everybody about how God has met *his* need during the week. I feel it would be improper not to let him have his say, but I feel restless as the interest of the group turns from me to Bill. To cover my restlessness I join the chorus of thanksgiving for what God has done for Bill. But my heart is not in the matter. My problems and blessings seem vastly more important than Bill's. The fellowship meeting has suddenly gone flat.

Why is it so hard for me to be interested in Bill's joys and sorrows? Can it be that I am looking to my fellow Christians for something I should really look to God for? It is true that God gave me their fellowship partly for my comfort, but perhaps I am leaning on them too much. For when God is my source of joy and comfort, I find I have more ability to give to the group than I have need to receive from it.

The rule must stand: *Look not every man on his own things*. The moment I find the rule hard to carry out, I know that the dry sponge which is my heart is sucking too greedily for the love of those around me. It cannot be squeezed to give forth sweetness. It needs to be heavy with the love of God, yielding its refreshment to the slightest pressure from my fellow Christians. As I find my joys in him, so my capacity to give will exceed my need to receive.

THAT WE ALL MAY BE ONE

It is not possible to exaggerate the importance of your fellowship with your fellow Christians. You need their love. You need their discipline. They need yours.

The gospel was preached to you not primarily in order that you might be delivered from the torments of hell but that you might be brought into simultaneous fellowship with God and with your brothers and sisters. Such, at least, is the teaching of 1 John 1:3-4. Such also was the burden of Christ's high priestly prayer in John 17.

Hours before his arrest and crucifixion, Jesus was pleading for the church of future ages. His vision encompassed you and me, and situations in which we, as Christians, find ourselves. Curiously, when he addressed himself to the church of the future, his requests were limited to one (Jn 17:20-23). He prayed only that we might be united, not organizationally but in heart. "I in them and thou in me, that they may become perfectly one, so that the world may know that thou hast sent me and hast loved them even as thou hast loved me" (Jn 17:23).

The fact that he made only one request for the church of the future indicates the importance of what he asked for. Yet as we look at the nature of his request, we wonder why unity of spirit should merit such exclusive attention. Had he prayed, for example, that the church might constantly be filled with the power of the Holy Spirit, it would make more sense to us. A zealous church, a church faithful to death, a church that could confound its foes: all these we could have understood. But a church in which the members enjoyed harmony and closeness in Christ among themselves, how important is it?

He gives us a repeated clue to the puzzle. "That the world may believe" is the phrase he uses in verse 21. The church was left on earth for that purpose: that the world might believe. Power in testimony is evidently not something that the church can possess as a sort of separate package; it cannot exist alone. The church that convinces others that there is a God in heaven is a church that manifests what only a heavenly God can do, that is, to unite human beings in heavenly love. Wherever the sign of loving unity exists, the world will be convinced. Miracles of healing, large mass rallies, powerful preaching and superb organization all may have their place. But there is nothing on earth that convinces humans about heaven or that awakens their craving for it like the discovery of Christians who love one another.

The power of advertising is enormous. In three months a large company can knock a smaller one out of business by mounting a massive advertising campaign. Political candidates who can be marketed effectively stand more chance of being elected. Christian organizations, bemused by the magic of advertising, bow down and worship the gods of Madison Avenue. But there are limits to what you can do with advertising. You may go on selling your product, but it will be sold to a cynical, disillusioned market who buy because there's nothing else they know about. And they *have* to buy something.

The problem is that too often the gospel is "marketed" and "bought" in this same spirit.

What are you going to do? You can't change the whole church, but you can begin in your own life to be an answer to the high priestly prayer of Christ. You can become a small focus of change. If you are willing to be a channel of unity, you will find the power of heaven on your side. Not only will you experience pains and joys of an order you had not dreamed possible, but you will become the scent of life to non-Christians around you. The sight of loving unity among believers arrests unbelievers. It crashes through the barriers of their intellect, stirs up their conscience and creates a tumult of longing in their heart. They were created to enjoy the very thing you are demonstrating.

I will not conclude this chapter with a Bible study. By all means look up the passages I have referred to. But let me leave you with the prayer of Francis of Assisi. Learn it by heart. Pray it from your heart. Become a focus of God's peace among the harassed Christians you associate with.

> Lord, make me an instrument of thy peace.
> Where there is hatred let me sow love;
> where there is injury, pardon;
> where there is doubt, faith;
> where there is despair, hope;
> where there is darkness, light; and
> where there is sadness, joy.

O Divine Master, grant that I may
not so much seek to be consoled as to console;
to be understood as to understand;
to be loved as to love;
for it is in giving that we receive;
it is in pardoning that we are pardoned; and
it is in dying that we are born to eternal life.

8

Guidance

People the world over cry out for personal guidance. Millions scan horoscope columns daily, searching for soundings to navigate the day's treacherous waters. Christians may search the Scriptures but are often bewildered, uncertain alike of chart and compass.

Their anxiety may lead them to the borders of superstition. When I was a boy, I mingled with Christians who went in for *promise boxes*. Inside the boxes were tiny rolls of paper that could be extracted with a pair of tweezers. As the box was passed round the room, you pulled out your scroll (much like the ones in Chinese fortune cookies) and unrolled it to read a Bible verse plus a religious rhyme.

"That's just for me!" someone would cry as the box was passed from hand to hand. "That's the very message I needed for today!"

I was only young, but something about the whole process of fitting the words on the little scroll to my own life seemed to increase my anxiety rather than diminish it.

Though few Christians are so naive in their attempts to find guidance, many are uneasy and uncertain, longing not only for guidance itself but for a clear understanding of how God gives direction.

It is strange that it should be so, for God is described as doing all he can to guide us. Such is the constant theme of the Psalms. "He shall be our guide eternally" (Ps 48:14 NEB). "I will teach you, and guide you in the way you should go. I will keep you under my eye" (Ps 32:8 NEB).

Before leaving his disciples Jesus was at pains to reassure them that the Holy Spirit would be a faithful and invaluable guide to them. "He will guide you into all truth" (Jn 16:13 NEB). It is strange in view of the repeated reassurances in the Bible of God's readiness to guide that his children should be so confused and anxious about the subject.

THE GENERAL NATURE OF GUIDANCE

Though the Bible never uses the word *guidance*, it does talk about a Guide. You may seek guidance, but God desires to give something better: himself. The point is profound. It's more than a play on words.

Deep in your heart it's a Guide, even more than guidance, that you want. Which would you prefer to have while driving in heavy traffic through a strange city, a complicated set of instructions from someone on the sidewalk or a kindly stranger who says, "Look, I'm on my way there right now. If you'll let me hop in, I'll show you the way"? For you as a Christian, guidance is meant to be an aspect of your ongoing relationship with God. He wants you to know him. Being guided by him is part of that.

Already you must have perceived that there are at least two

elements in guidance that are inseparable in experience: direction and support. I may inquire about Smith Street. On the surface I am requesting a set of directions. But beneath the surface I am anxious. I am lost. My uncertainty about where I am, whether I can get where I want to in time, whether I can understand and follow directions accurately all make me crave reassurance.

"My sheep hear my voice," says Jesus, "and I know them, and they follow me" (Jn 10:27). It is not only direction but also the reassurance of his presence that is promised. "My presence will go with you, and I will give you rest" God told Moses (Ex 33:14).

"How very infantalizing," some of my psychiatric colleagues would respond. "Christians seem to be reduced to perpetual dependency. They never become mature enough to take responsibility for their personal decisions. Not only do they have to be told what to do, but they need someone who will hold their hand while they do it."

Dependency? Yes. Infantalization? No. Like all human beings you are basically dependent, you were created to be so. Humans were never meant to have the kind of maturity that makes them independent of God. Through all eternity you will bow the knee to him and rejoice over the sweet comfort of his presence.

But you will mature. Although maturity and the capacity to be independent are related, they are not synonymous. As you mature, both the kind of relationship you have with God and the type of guidance you will require of him will change. You will grow more loving and trusting. You will more often *know*, without needing to ask, what he would have you do, because you will know him and the manner of his thoughts.

In order to understand how this can be so, you must grasp two things about the nature of divine guidance: First, God has an overall goal for your life; second, God's goal is a moral goal. His plan for you has less to do with geography than with ethics. His supreme object is to make you like his Child (Rom 8:29). Whether the process of making what he wants of you involves travel, money, joy, pain or whatever is secondary. His goal is to make you holy, and the kind of guidance he will give you will reflect this.

It is precisely at this point that you may have problems. Usually when we want guidance, we have in the back of our minds some overall objective toward which we are striving. I may ask you to direct me to Smith Street, but my real object is to find a certain doctor who can cure me of cancer. Similarly I may want to know whether I should apply for job A or job B, but in the back of my mind I am really struggling with vague goals that have to do with happiness, success or even money.

Thus when we ask God for guidance, we may have one goal in mind while he has another. We may not therefore be interested in the kind of guidance he has to offer.

It is not that the two *kinds* of goal (geographical and moral) are unrelated. Geography and ethics go together. Generally when I want to decide between Chicago and New York, there will be some moral aspect to my decision. Perhaps I promised to go to New York, but it will be more financially rewarding to go to Chicago. And if I may put it this simply, God is less worried about whether I make a mistake about the geography than about the morality. It matters less that I wind up in the wrong city than that I make a wrong moral choice.

SCRIPTURE AND GUIDANCE

I mustn't give you the impression that it will be simple to figure out the morality of all your decisions. In the first place there may not seem to be too much morality involved. Even when there is, it may be confusing to decide where right lies or what your deepest motives are. If it were simple to understand the right and wrong of our everyday living, you would not need the weighty volume of Holy Writ or the promptings and illumination of the Holy Spirit to understand them.

Here indeed lies your most pressing need for guidance: The need to distinguish right from wrong in everyday living. "How can a young man keep his way pure?" inquires the psalmist. "By guarding it according to thy word. . . . I have laid up thy word in my heart, that I might not sin against thee" (Ps 119:9, 11).

The Bible must not be used as a horoscope. I cannot deny that many Christians, while they are reading the Bible, have been peculiarly gripped by a particular sentence or verse that has served as the voice of God speaking directly to them. But I do contend that such experiences are not the norm. God does not desire to guide us magically. He wants us to know his mind. He wants us to grasp his very heart. We need minds so soaked with the content of Scripture, so imbued with biblical outlooks and principles, so sensitive to the Holy Spirit's prompting that we will know instinctively the upright step to take in any circumstance, small or great.

Therefore the most important use of Scripture is that through studying it you may become acquainted with the ways and thoughts of God. The Bible is not a celestial Ouija board.

But you will say, "Doesn't the Bible speak of visions, dreams, prophecies, voices and all sorts of special interventions?" Indeed, it does. "Do these things still happen?" Undoubtedly. And I have personally experienced some of them.

But pause to think for a moment. Many of the dramatic, "special" types of guidance were given to people who were too set on their own ways. This can be said of Pharaoh, Moses, Balaam, Peter, Nebuchadnezzar, Paul and many others. In other instances the guidance was of so exceptional a nature that nothing less than a vision would serve, or the people had so little knowledge of God that they could be reached in no other way. God has something better in mind so far as your everyday walk is concerned.

His aim is that you become his companion, that you walk together with him. He already knows all about you. Now he wants you to understand something of him. The more you understand of him, the more real the companionship will be and the more likely you are to keep in step with him in the direction he is taking you.

THE PERSUASIVE POWER OF DESIRE

It is one thing to know how God thinks. It is quite another to want what he wants. And our wants have an uncanny way of influencing our thoughts and opinions.

I remember an unmarried woman missionary who fell in love with a divorced colleague. The man concerned had previously maintained that though he saw no scriptural objection to remarriage, he would never contemplate it. She, on the other hand, saw remarriage following divorce as wrong—until the two of them fell in love. Then her ingenuity in finding scriptural support for their marriage excited my admiration.

The point at issue is not the morality of remarriage after divorce so much as the strange power that strong attraction has over previously held opinions and intentions. Since we are all made of the same clay, we share this same tendency. Not only are we at odds with God, but we allow our desires to color our thinking. It would be simple if only we consistently desired the opposite of what God wanted. In that case guidance would consist of doing all the things we hated and of avoiding everything we liked. God's will would be easy enough to follow, but hardly pleasant.

Yet the fact is that many of our desires are seeds of God's own planting. We are tossed about in swirling eddies of godly and ungodly wishes until we are confused and dizzy and lose our bearings.

Often in my practice as a psychiatrist I meet conscientious Christians who feel that if they want something really badly, it goes without saying that it is not God's will. God's favorite word is no and his favorite pastime, doing without. He is the God of thunder and ice.

Who will liberate our minds from the bondage of our wishes? If my mind is at the mercy of my passions, how can I ever use it to distinguish between godly and ungodly wishes? Or, as someone put the question to me recently, "How can I know when I pray for guidance that I am not just talking myself into doing what I want anyway?"

Before I attempt to resolve our dilemma, let me throw in one last difficulty. Half the time when we need guidance, we don't know what our true desires are. Indeed, for one reason or another, we may be hiding from them. Sigmund Freud is reported to have told friends that when he had a difficult decision to make it was his practice to flip a coin. To their astonished inquiries he replied, "If when the coin comes down and I am pleased, then I know what it was I *really* wanted. If on the other hand I am disappointed, I am clearer as to what *I don't want* to do."

It may be, then, that before I ask the question, What does God want? I should ask the prior question, What do I want? Until I have scrutinized my desires, how can I measure the sway they hold over the theater of my mind? Let them be called into full view. "Search me, O God, and know my heart: try me and know my thoughts."

Perhaps when they are hauled from their hiding places, God will smile at them and say, "I wondered when you were going to bring me that one." Or I may discover flaws and defects on observing a desire in fuller light, defects that are out of keeping with the deepest longing of my life. In that case, because I have seen it for what it is, I may find myself able to throw the desire away, becoming light and free in the process.

All would be hopeless if we had to do with a God who didn't care. But happily God is more anxious to guide us than we are to be guided. He is perpetually active, gently penetrating our defenses and setting us free from the slavery of our hidden wishes. The problem of guidance resolves itself into collaborating with our Guide and Liberator.

GUIDANCE AND GIFTS

When I talk about holiness, I must be careful not to make you see it in negative terms. Note that God's goal for you is not that you merely *avoid* certain things. Holiness is a positive quality which cannot be divorced from your everyday living. An activity may be holy or unholy according to the motive and spirit in which it is carried out. Holiness allows for the fullest expression of your bodily appetites and your natural and spiritual gifts.

Our tendency is to label certain activities holy and others secular. To go to a prayer meeting is spiritual. To play the piano is, well, it's OK. But it's qualitatively different, and it's certainly less important. Or so we judge.

But going to a prayer meeting can be highly unspiritual if I go in bitterness and unbelief. And playing the piano can be good or bad according to the spirit in which I play. The question is important since it bears on what kind of occupation you will wind up in. Is God's goal of making you Christlike consistent with a career as a concert pianist? Can you be a Christlike member of the armed forces? Or a business executive? Is every "secular" occupation either second best or frankly suspect, and would all Christians be better off being in "Christian work"?

It will not be long before you discover that certain "full-time" Christian workers, while hesitating modestly to come right out and say so, emit verbal and nonverbal signals that tell us they believe that only full-time Christian service is in the center of God's will. Only the "professionals" (those who gain their living by the gospel) are really *in*, the rest of us being second-class citizens. Sometimes we even see ourselves as such.

Not all professionals would go this far. Yet in favor of the view is the clear fact that many Christian professionals have truly faced the question of treasure on earth versus treasure in heaven and have chosen a pathway of sacrifice and faith, something which cannot be said nearly so frequently of the rest of us. But the dichotomy is artificial. If any distinction should be made among Christians, it should be on the basis of the degree of commitment and faith to Christ, not on full-time versus part-time status.

All of us are meant to be full time in the sense that all we do is to be done to the glory of God. And if God has imparted natural abilities to us, we should think very seriously before deciding not to develop and use them. The question really is: Can I best serve God by earning my living and employing my natural gifts (and bearing witness among my colleagues) or by devoting all my time to Christian work and sacrificing the use of some of my other abilities? Sometimes there are clear-cut answers to the question. The ability to undress teasingly does not call for a career as a Christian striptease artist.

Up to now I have been talking about natural abilities, things God gave me by inheritance, background or training, but which are not supernatural in nature. Before drawing the threads together we should look briefly at what Scripture teaches about supernatural or spiritual gifts. These are special abilities imparted supernaturally by the Holy Spirit to Christians to enable the church to function adequately. Just as your body requires the functions of your liver, heart, kidneys, muscles and even your toenails, so also members of the church have complementary roles and abilities enabling the church to function as a working organism. And since the role of the church is essentially supernatural, it follows that the most important gifts in its functioning will be spiritual rather than natural ones.

Not all Christians are in agreement as to whether all the gifts still are meant to operate today. Be this as it may, God desires you to have spiritual gifts, and he makes it clear that some are more important than others.

To what extent am I to be guided about my occupation in life by the gifts that God has given me? Obviously, God-given gifts, whether natural or spiritual, are not to be despised. They were entrusted to me to develop and use. For some Christians no conflict arises. In their lives they give fullest expression to both natural and supernatural abilities. But since God is generous in imparting gifts, some Christians are forced to decide which they will concentrate on.

As a young physician, Dr. D. Martyn Lloyd Jones was a cardiologist of exceptional caliber, serving as assistant to Lord Horder, physician to the British royal family. Yet God had also given him supernatural gifts as an expositor of Scripture and as a prophetic voice in the church. It was impossible for him to find time for the fullest expression of both his medical and his Christian gifts. He chose the latter and preached in a small Presbyterian church in Wales. Later, from the pulpit of Westminster Chapel in London, he influenced the whole evangelical movement in Britain, and through his many books and lectures was respected and loved throughout the world.

Therefore bring not only your desires but also your gifts and abilities before the Lord as you contemplate how you will serve him in the future. Remember that a God-given gift is never to be despised, though it may have to be neglected where circumstances call for the exercise of more important gifts. And as a general rule I might suggest that where the full exercise of a natural ability comes into conflict with the full exercise of a spiritual gift, the former should be sacrificed to the latter.

COUNSEL, CIRCUMSTANCES AND FLEECES

You will notice that so far I have given you no simple formula for being guided. Neither our wishes nor our gifts are conclusive, infallible criteria. Nor are counsel, circumstances or fleeces.

Fleeces. Let me dispose of the least important first. If you have never heard of fleeces, skip the next three paragraphs.

Gideon, a young Israelite, had a vision calling him to deliver Israel. After praying about the matter, he used a "fleece of wool" as a means of confirming God's will (Judg 6:36-40). Gideon's fleece has become the basis of a practice among some Christians which is called "putting out a fleece." In essence, when you put out a fleece you say to God, "If you really want me to carry out plan A, then please make the telephone ring at 9:10 p.m., then I will know that plan A is what you want." (You can make the "fleece" anything you wish, just so long as it can serve as a "sign" to you.)

I feel not only that it is inappropriate for Christians to behave like a semipagan (Gideon's home was a center of idolatry [Judg 6:25-26]), but that it is also inappropriate for them to design crude experiments in which God is part of the experiment. I'm sure Christians don't realize what they are doing, but this is indeed what it boils down to. Please God, jump into my box and perform. If the Word of God is not enough for you, fleeces will also leave you in doubt. You are looking in the wrong direction for guidance, and you will be left floundering.

Forget about fleeces. If you've never used them, don't start. If you have, then quit.

Counsel. In seeking counsel from someone older and wiser, you are on more solid ground. When you look for counsel, however, there are certain ground rules. First, don't choose someone because you know they will tell you what you want to hear. Choose someone who seems wise enough and mature enough to be able to point out some aspect of your problem that you may not have taken into account. Second, don't go with the idea of letting your mentor make the decision for you. You want a firsthand relationship with God. The decision must be yours. Don't even allow yourself to worry about the approval of the person you talk to. You are going to have to answer to God, not to your counselor.

The value of counsel lies in the additional data available to you as well as the different perspective. It would be so comforting if the counselor could tell you what to do, but you may have to go against his or her advice. This doesn't mean that you will have wasted your time, for it is never a waste of time to think through all aspects of a problem carefully. Nevertheless the responsibility before God rests with you. If others could make your decision for you, you could blame them if things went wrong. Seek counsel by all means, but let the responsibility of deciding on the will of God be yours.

Circumstances. Circumstances may or may not be a guide as to what you should do. If you have an umbrella and it starts to rain, you will not need special guidance to use it. If the house is cold, turn up the thermostat.

But circumstances alone can never guide the Christian. A door may be locked and marked "Keep Out," but these circumstances are not enough. If someone were lying injured on the other side of the door, you would be justified in breaking it down to help the person inside.

When we speak of circumstances, we are talking only about those circumstances we *perceive*. There may be other circumstances unknown to us that would alter the whole picture. When Jesus made his last journey to Jerusalem, his disciples protested that the circumstances pointed against his going. He would face extreme danger. But Jesus took into account other circumstances that the disciples could not even contemplate. He went knowing that he would be crucified and that his death would provide a ransom for sinners.

What it boils down to is that it would be far easier for us to know what to do if we knew all the circumstances. But since we never do, we will in practice make some sound decisions *in spite of* known circumstances and others *because of* them.

You might conclude that circumstances are of no help to you in deciding the will of God, but you are wrong. It is always good to look at them squarely if for no other reason than to count the cost of your decision. But circumstances can never be the sole criterion. Circumstances should be given less weight than morality.

THE VOICE OF THE SHEPHERD

Sooner or later you will meet Christians who say, "I felt led to do such and such." Or "My friends criticize me for what I am doing, but I have real peace about it." Sometimes you will be favorably impressed, and at other times you may wonder whether the person speaking is making God an excuse for doing exactly what he or she wanted. At any rate you will have stumbled across the thorny problem of *subjectivism*. The leading of the Spirit, inner peace, a sense of reassurance: all have to do with subjective feelings. How do I interpret my feelings? If I feel a strong urge to telephone a friend, how can I know whether the urge comes from God or from my muddled psyche?

Some Christians warn us against paying heed to our feelings. They prefer to go by objective criteria, the plain teaching of God's Word, circumstances and others. They have been driven to this position because of their disillusionment with the way other Christians abuse subjective elements in guidance.

I remember once being confronted by a group of earnest Christians who described to me a course of action they "felt led" to take. I felt that the action was unscriptural and morally wrong. "But you don't seem to realize, John," came the answer, "that we spent a whole weekend fasting and praying about it. We *know* God is leading us." The implication was plain enough: two days of fasting and prayer guaranteed that they were right. If my interpretation of Scripture made their actions seem wrong, who was I to differ with God's leading?

Unfortunately it is not so simple as my friends thought. It is just as possible to "psych" myself into believing something I want to during two days of fasting and prayer as it is to do so in an hour. "The heart is deceitful above all things and desperately wicked." Once again we are facing the problem of dominance of our conscious and unconscious wishes.

If you have an inner urge to do something that contradicts Scripture, you may be sure that the urge is not from God. Yet Christian experience must not be reduced to following a set of written instructions.

Scripture emphasizes the presence of a Guide rather than techniques for being guided. "My presence will go with you, and I will give you rest." We are meant to enjoy the subjective experiences of comfort, reassurance and fellowship with God. The fact that some Christians allow themselves to be deceived, confusing the voice of their own desires with the voice of the Shepherd, must not make us retreat from the assertion that God has promised guidance as well as the experience of fellowship with him while he is guiding us. Yet if other Christians can be fooled, what is to prevent me from being fooled?

When Jesus said, "My sheep hear my voice," we correctly interpret him to say, "My sheep can distinguish my voice." But that is not all he was saying. The word used implies "My sheep *pay heed to* my voice." The sheep is not concerned about losing the way. The shepherd knows the right way and will make sure the sheep is taken care of. What does concern the sheep is that the commands are obeyed. If I but concern myself with *hearing the voice of the Shepherd*, paying heed to Christ, obeying him, doing his will, I shall find that the problem of distinguishing his voice will begin to take care of itself. So will the problem of losing my way in life.

And is not this the fear that paralyzes us, the fear of missing our way so that we cannot take a step lest we be deceived? "I dare not move," you cry. "My heart is so deceitful. It is so possible for me to fool myself. It is better for me to take no step at all than to take a wrong step." At this point you may make your most serious blunder. You can't follow Christ if you stand still. It is often better to make a mistake than not to move at all.

At the back of your mind you may feel that following Christ is like walking a tightrope. One false move and you're done for. Yet if the sheep strays a little, the shepherd will not abandon him or her. He will call the sheep, and if the sheep fails to respond to the call, he will fetch him or her. Guidance is not walking a tightrope.

I don't encourage you to stray or to take a wrong path in life or to presume on the goodness of the Shepherd. But I do encourage you not to feel condemned to a second-rate life if you miss the way at some point. God is not primarily concerned with whether you wind up in Brooklyn or Bangkok so much as with your relationship with himself.

Learning to be guided is in any case like learning to sail. Recently I bought a Laser, a fast but rather tippy little sailboat. The winds where I sail veer frequently and are gusty. I found the Laser much more of a challenge than the more stable boats I had previously sailed. In learning to handle the boat I would capsize as many as ten times in one afternoon. But gradually I got the feel of the boat and it fairly hummed as it skimmed over the waves.

Being guided is like learning to sail. At first staying upright is more important than reaching your final destination. If you find yourself floundering under water beneath an upturned boat, it is all part of the fun, however alarming it may seem the first few times. Then little by little as you learn how to make the boat respond to different winds, you can take a more intelligent interest in your destination.

In the same way, God's object is to teach you how to be guided. You *will* capsize from time to time—but no matter. Capsizing is part of learning.

PREREQUISITES FOR GUIDANCE

There is no simple formula for getting God's guidance. Since you never know all the *circumstances*, you may sometimes have to ignore those you do know. Your *gifts* usually, but not necessarily, have a bearing on your vocation. It is wise to seek *advice*, but sometimes you will have to go against it. Your *inward desires* may or may not point you in the direction God would have you go. *Subjective sensations* may represent the Spirit leading or your own self-will. Only *moral laws* serve as unchanging guides to conduct.

How then can you be guided? It seems to me that what you need is not a formula but an attitude, an attitude with three related components:

1. You must share God's outlook.

2. You must will God's will.

3. You must trust God.

By *sharing God's outlook* I mean that you must adopt God's priorities. In doing so you will become more concerned about making an *upright* decision rather than a *right* decision; you will be more concerned about righteousness than about geography and about sanctity more than salary.

Obviously you will be better equipped to discern God's will the more you know about Scripture. Yet a knowledge of Scripture in itself will not help you. What you need is an attitude that so values the truth of Scripture that your chief aim will be to put its truth into practice.

So study Scripture. Memorize it. Meditate on it. But do all this with the aim of finding how to live a life that pleases God. In this way your mind will be predisposed to understand the will of God more easily in a specific circumstance. In a sense you will already have begun to will God's will.

By *willing God's will* I mean choosing it deliberately by an act of your own will. It is a decision to accept God's will even though it may conflict with your personal longing. Insofar as you may not know the specific *content* of God's will, you are making a blind choice. Yet insofar as you know God himself, your choice is not blind. You know the *character* and the *competence* of the person whose will you choose.

The choice may lie between what you want and what God wants. On the one hand the two "wants" may coincide. But on the other they may not. In the case of a conflict of interests you are electing God's way in preference to your own.

There is nothing particularly virtuous about making such a

decision. Since God loves you and is all-knowing, it makes sense to prefer his plan to your own. Nevertheless the decision to will his will may hurt, in part, because it means adopting his values and priorities that you do not automatically share.

The third component which contributes to an attitude conducive to guidance has to do with faith. In order to understand what I mean by *trusting God*, we will have to look first at the reasons why doubts and misgivings arise about his guidance. It seems to me there are two basically different kinds of doubt. First, you may doubt that God's will really is better than your own. Your own is something you understand and you feel safe with. Second, you may question your own capacity to interpret guidance.

It sounds ridiculous to say that you would doubt that God's will is better. Though in theory we never question it, in practice we often do. It is one thing to believe that water can support your body. It is quite another (if you are a nonswimmer) to abandon yourself to the weird sensation of sink-float disorientation you experience in the water. In practice we do as the nonswimmer does. We retreat rapidly to something we have trusted in the past (putting feet on the bottom, grabbing the side rail, hanging on to someone). Mentally we freeze, blocking out of our minds any other possibility than the familiar one. Common sense flies away in the face of anxiety.

Our fears about the will of God make us freeze in the same way. We cling to the side rails rather than risk the unknown. It is one thing to believe in the intellectual proposition of a loving, omnipotent God. It is quite another to entrust our destinies to him. We grow anxious and fearful as we become aware of how much hangs in the balance. We close our minds to what God would say, understanding only what we have already experienced.

> Trust in the LORD with all your heart,
> and do not rely on your own insight.
> In all your ways acknowledge him,
> and he will make straight your paths. (Prov 3:5-6)

Therefore when you seek guidance, search your heart for anxiety. What makes you so concerned to get the "right" guidance? If you have a personal preference for one particular way, does your preference indicate a fear of trusting God? If so, face your fear. Drag it into his presence and tell him you will trust him whatever he calls you to do.

The second kind of fear is more perplexing. How can you be sure that you are being led by God and not misled by your own desires? Who can understand his or her own heart? You can cope with losing money, being in danger and risk to your family. You will face all of these things and more just so long as you can be sure that God is leading you. It is this—the assurance of a true relationship with God in a specific decision—that you crave. If you can be sure of this, you will make any decision, however much others might misunderstand or criticize you, or whatever hardships you might be called on to face. But how can you be sure?

Only by faith. Only by faith can you know that God is more concerned to guide you than you are to be guided, that by your mistakes he will teach you to go in the right direction as well as how to distinguish his voice. Only by faith can you have any assurance about anything. If you are trusting him for your eternal destiny already, is it such a big matter to trust him for guidance now?

You say, "I don't trust *myself*." Precisely. You are not called on to trust yourself but to trust in the Lord. You have neither the discernment nor the purity of motive to merit guidance. But guidance is given, not earned. You will never merit it. Therefore you must trust God to give it to you. You must trust *his* generosity, *his* ability to get through to you, *his* power to pull you up short when you go wrong, *his* ability to teach you the sound of his voice.

Take courage, then, when you have a tough decision to make. Someone who cares deeply for you already knows what he wants you to do. He takes delight in having fellowship with you and wants the very circumstances you face to draw you closer to him.

For him, the thing you call guidance is not a perplexing problem but a means whereby he may draw closer to you. It would make good sense for you to adopt the same perspective.

PASSAGES TO STUDY

1. Read Psalm 25:1-4.

    *   The word *guidance* is nowhere found in this passage. Yet in several verses the idea of being directed by God occurs. Find the verses and note the expressions used for guidance.

    *   What evidence is there (if any) to support my contention that God is primarily interested in the moral aspect of guidance?

    *   List the qualities found in one who will receive God's guidance. In particular, what degree of moral perfection does God demand *before* he will guide? (See v. 8.)

Note. Though the word *fear* in the Bible does mean "fear," and even "terror," in this particular context it connotes profound reverence and respect.

2. Read James 1:5-7.

   • Your study of Psalm 25 may have led you to conclude that you will have to merit guidance by achieving a certain spiritual posture before God. What expressions in this passage would dispel such a notion?

   • What prerequisite to guidance does James emphasize?

9

Holiness

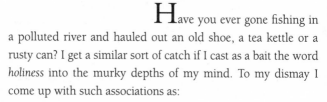

Have you ever gone fishing in a polluted river and hauled out an old shoe, a tea kettle or a rusty can? I get a similar sort of catch if I cast as a bait the word *holiness* into the murky depths of my mind. To my dismay I come up with such associations as:

- hollow-eyed gauntness
- beards
- long robes and sandals
- stone cells
- no sex
- no jokes
- hair shirts
- frequent cold baths
- fasting
- getting up at 4 a.m. to pray
- self-humiliation

The list is a strange one. Some items suggest you can only achieve holiness by a painful and rigorous process. Yet many teachers claim that your most intense efforts will be vain since holiness is something God gives, not something you achieve. Again, my juxtaposition of items lends an air of frivolity to a subject which none of us dare take lightly. If the means by which men and women have sought holiness seem ridiculous, we should weep rather than laugh.

More important, my mental flotsam and jetsam point to something unreal in our views of holiness. Take the items robes, sandals, beard. We picture Jesus so. Hence, while consciously aware that his robes and beard have little to do with his holiness, we unconsciously lump them all together. If you doubt what I say, try to picture Jesus with a moustache, wearing blue jeans and riding a bicycle. If you are anything like most of us, you will be shocked even though you are aware intellectually that there is nothing unholy about jeans or bikes, and no moral reason why Jesus would not in the twenty-first century make use of either of them.

Our paradoxical reactions are a clue to artificiality in our thinking about holiness and about God's Holy One. For while in one sense holiness has to do with the "wholly Other," it yet must penetrate to the most mundane of our daily activities so that the division between sacred and secular vanishes entirely from our lives.

THE GOD WHO IS HOLY

Two ideas are paramount when the Bible talks about God's holiness, an attribute which more than any other seems to express the essence of what God is. One idea has to do with separateness and difference. God is wholly unlike anything we can conceive or know. He is infinitely greater and more powerful, besides being qualitatively utterly dissimilar from us and from the universe he created. Though we are made in his image, and therefore reflect his being, the difference is such as to create a chasm of endless depth between what he is and what we are. "I am what I am," says God, "and there is nothing with which I can be compared."

The second idea has to do with morality. Bound up in the qualitative difference I have mentioned is ultimate ethical beauty and moral perfection. God's holiness is not merely total separation from uncleanness but a positive goodness beyond our capacity to conceive. The very heavens are unclean in his sight. Yet it is this same goodness and beauty that he wants to share with you. He wants you to be like him.

You will never understand him, yet you are called to know him. You are different from him, yet he wants to give you the quality which most distinguishes him from you. *You are redeemed to be set aside for God's special use and made a partaker of his moral perfection.*

Knowing him and sharing his holiness are closely related. "Who shall ascend the hill of the LORD? And who shall stand in his holy place? He who has clean hands and a pure heart" (Ps 24:3-4). Only pure eyes can see him, and that but dimly. Yet if you but catch a glimpse of him, he will share his beauty with you so that your face, like that of Moses, will shine with glory.

Holiness is not optional for the Christian. It is not an elective. It is your major. The command rings out from across the yawning gulf, "Be ye holy for I am holy." Impossible as the command may seem, you have no choice but to obey it. "This is the will of

God, your sanctification" (1 Thess 4:3). You are left with no say in the matter. It is the will of God that you be holy, and be holy you must (Rom 6:22; 12:1; Eph 1:4; 1 Thess 3:13; 4:7; 2 Tim 1:9; 1 Pet 1:15; 2:5; 2 Pet 3:11). But how?

PEACE AND HOLINESS

Now for a little theology. When you became a Christian, God did much more than forgive your sins. *He made you righteous.* He, the judge of dead and living, pronounced you, "Not guilty!" He now looks upon you and behaves toward you as though you were perfectly righteous. He does not deceive himself about you. Rather, your hand is held by the hand of the Christ who redeemed you by his blood. "This one is mine!" Jesus cries. "I have paid for every one of her transgressions." "It is well!" the reply comes back from the throne. "For such as her I sent you to suffer. Henceforth let there be peace between her and me. Welcome, ransomed child of mine; your sins are blotted out as the sun by a thick cloud. I will remember them no more."

The process by which you were pronounced righteous and by which your peace was made with God is called justification. "Therefore, since we are *justified* by faith, we have *peace with God* through our Lord Jesus Christ" (Rom 5:1).

But God did more than justify you. He *sanctified you.* Not content with declaring you righteous, he began to share his holiness with you. "Not with *me*," you may say. "I only wish I could be sanctified. It is one thing to know I am justified. It is quite another to claim I am sanctified." Yet the Scriptures insist on both. They are two sides of the same coin. Unless you grasp their intimate relationship, you will enjoy neither the peace of justification nor the joy and freedom of sanctification. To separate them is to mutilate both. Consider the following verses.

To the proud and compromising Corinthian church Paul writes, "He [God] is the source of your life in Christ Jesus, whom God made our wisdom, our righteousness and sanctification and redemption" (1 Cor 1:30). Again, "For their sakes I sanctify myself," states Jesus, "that they also might be sanctified through the truth" (Jn 17:19 KJV). "Christ loved the church and gave himself up for her, that he might sanctify her, having cleansed her by the washing of water with the word" (Eph 5:25-26). Christ "gave himself for us to redeem us from all iniquity and to purify for himself a people of his own who are zealous for good deeds" (Tit 2:14). "He himself bore our sins in his body on the tree, that we might die to sin and live to righteousness" (1 Pet 2:24). Notice how intimately sanctification, redemption and justification are linked together. No hint here of separation. Check the verses again to make sure. The separation exists in the minds of Christians, not in the pages of Scripture. Indeed the church in Hebrews is defined as "those who are sanctified" and Christ as "he who sanctifies" (Heb 2:11).

You may not have noticed my definition of sanctification a page or so back. God did two things when he sanctified you. By an operation of the Holy Spirit *he set you apart for his own exclusive use.* In addition he began a process within you to fit you for divine use. He began, by the Holy Spirit, to make you a holy person.

For many years I grappled with the problem of how I could live a holy life. I attended spiritual life conferences of different kinds in different countries and received conflicting counsels and various degrees of temporary help. I read every book I could lay my hands on about "victorious living." Often I would feel that I had turned a major corner in my life and would seem finally to be in possession of the secret of sanctification. But I could no more hang on to the secret than capture a sunbeam in my pocket. A few days after turning the latest corner I would repeat to myself the words that had conjured up the precious understanding, only to find that the words no longer had the same effect on me. The fizz had gone out of the pop. The "truth" had become flat, stale and unprofitable.

If the only result had been to produce in me a wistful acceptance of that which could never be, I might have remained content. But I lost my peace. I knew I was a Christian, yet I was crushed with a sense of guilt and failure. How could God be pleased with or accept someone who sinned so much as I?

During my years as a missionary a recurring dream symbolized my conflict. I would find myself surrounded by piles of medical books on the night before my final exam. In my dream I was frantically skimming through the books, attempting to absorb in one night the knowledge I should have been learning for years. Yet I knew my task was hopeless. I had opened only three or four books while scores remained untouched as the night wore inexorably on. Despair overwhelmed me. I would struggle against a suffocating sense of doom and wake up sweating, trembling and depressed.

What I failed to understand during those years was the intimate relationship between peace and holiness (or between justification and sanctification). At times light would begin to break as I read certain passages in the New Testament, but the passages never got the necessary grip on my mind. Only in later life did I discover with wonder that *sanctification arose out of justification, that holiness arose out of peace,* and that to separate the two was to mutilate both.

The late Bishop Ryle put the matter even more strongly.

> Both [peace and holiness] are to be found in the same persons. Those who are justified are always sanctified, and those who are sanctified are always justified. God has joined them together and they cannot be put asunder. Both begin at the same time. The moment a person begins to be justified, he also begins to be a sanctified person. He may not feel it, but it is a fact.[1]

Let me explain how the principle works out in my own life. Although I knew in my head that I was justified by faith, I rarely profited from the knowledge. I dragged my feet through life beneath a burden of guilt. Often I had little heart for common Christian duties because of a leaden sense of the impossibility of straightening out my life. How could I confess the same sin for the hundredth time? Where was my sincerity? Having gone through "sanctifying experiences" several times, having dedicated my all to Christ, having rested in him, yielded to the Holy Spirit and trusted God to work in me what I could never work in myself, my situation seemed hopeless.

Light began to break over me when I realized in the depths of my spirit that I was forgiven, cleansed, accepted, justified, *because of what Christ had done for me* and not because of the depth of my yieldedness. I had preached this gospel to non-Christians for twenty-five years but had never tasted its full sweetness. It was as though dawn broke. Suddenly the relief of knowing that I was forgiven and loved lifted the load off my spirit. I found that I was set free, free to be holy. To my astonishment I discovered that I wanted to live a holy life far more than I wanted to sin. Forgiveness freed me to do what I wanted most.

I cannot say my life has been sinless since then, only that now each time I am guilt-ridden, I return to the cross of our Lord Jesus. I go shamelessly. I do not struggle to experience feelings or to achieve the requisite degree of piety. I recognize that peace and forgiveness do not depend on feelings of piety but on Christ and what he has done. To the degree that by faith I praise God for Christ and his finished work, I find myself liberated anew to be holy. It was not that previous teaching had been wrong so much as that it never got to the root of my problem.

I have not arrived at perfect sanctification. What has happened is that I have begun an ongoing learning process. The nearest thing I can compare it to is learning to sail. We sail on a lake where the wind is gusty and veers frequently. I have capsized many times. But I am learning. It is something like learning to ride a bicycle in the middle of an earthquake, yet somehow I am beginning to harmonize with wind and water and sail. And if I am flung overboard as I capsize, I right the boat, get in again and sail on. I am covered from head to foot with bruises, but who cares? I'm becoming a sailor.

In the same way I am learning about holiness. At one time it was only in shame and humiliation that I went back to the cross for forgiveness. The humiliation included a lot of self-conceit. Now I go back gladly. It is the basic maneuver of holy living. Now, bruised and breathless, I scramble aboard my righted boat and sail on, praising my Redeemer. I am learning to sail. I am learning to be holy.

A new awareness of God's grace and compassion is affecting me. While it does not make sin seem less sinful, it has changed my whole attitude to conviction. Formerly when convicted, I would react with discouragement. Now I praise God. "Thank you for telling me, Lord" is my grateful and spontaneous reply. "How good you are to keep telling me." I have discovered that the Holy Spirit is like a sailing instructor quickly pointing to my faults so I might learn faster and capsize less frequently. More than this, the grace of his Spirit's conviction makes continuous fellowship with him easier. He does not convict to condemn me but to draw me back to himself. This makes for a moment-to-moment fellowship with God that is indescribably precious. I might forget him for hours, but when I remember, I marvel that he still pursues me and draws me back into loving communion again.

If you have any question about the close relationship between justification and sanctification consider the following facts:

1. When you were justified, for the first time certain things appeared to you as sin. Sanctification had begun. It affected your moral perceptions.

2. Immediately following your conversion, you probably found for a while that it was easier to overcome temptation. Set free from a sense of guilt, you were freed to walk in purity.

3. Following your justification, you had a new desire for righteousness and purity, and a stronger inclination to follow them. This took place because your sanctification had begun.

What you did not anticipate after so auspicious a beginning was the intense struggle and the dismal failures that came later. You failed to grasp the nature of struggle, not realizing that neither the Holy Spirit nor your sinful tendencies would ever reach a compromise.

You were justified and you were sanctified. The question is: What went wrong with the sanctifying process? How may it be reestablished?

CRISIS OR GROWTH?

All of life combines both crises and periods of growth. Birth is a crisis. Weaning is a crisis. Puberty, adolescence, marriage and the firstborn child are all periods of crisis dividing long periods of less spectacular development.

Sanctification too has its crises. There are moments of new insight about areas in my life the Spirit needs to clean up, clearer visions into how I may collaborate with God in the ongoing work of sanctification.

However, not all crises in the Christian life are God produced. Some are preacher produced and spurious. And about one thing we must be especially clear: There is no crisis (except that of Christian conversion) that *can* produce sanctification. You began to be sanctified when you placed your faith in Christ. At that very time God set you apart for his special use. He also began a process in you designed to fit you for that use and to impart holiness to you.

It may be that the process, because of your unfaithfulness or your misunderstanding, has ground to a halt. If so, there is no delay at God's end. The Holy Spirit is ready to get on with his part. You do not need to wait until you can go to a special convention. Turn now to Romans 12:1-2.

> I appeal to you therefore, brethren, by the mercies of God, to present your bodies as a living sacrifice, holy and acceptable to God, which is your spiritual worship. Do not be conformed to this world but be transformed by the renewal of your mind, that you may prove what is the will of God, what is good and acceptable and perfect.

Why do you need to present your body? Because although

God *made* your body and is its owner/creator, and although he *redeemed* your body, he will never force you to give it to him. He has every right to it, yet he wants you to give it to him freely. Now. By an act of your will. And he wants you to go on remembering that your body belongs to him and behave accordingly.

If in the rush of life old habits of thought reassert themselves and you forget, waste no time mourning your failure but say, "Thank you for reminding me, Lord. My body is yours to do with as you please. Forgive me for failing—but I always will apart from you." And in so presenting your body you will have presented your time, your intelligence, your volition and every-thing you are. You have also opened your being to being filled with the Holy Spirit.

You will not be doing anything epoch-making. Your body has been his all along. All that is happening is that God, by his Spirit, will take up the process of sanctification where it left off.

"Do not be conformed to this world, but be transformed." Transformation is not an overnight matter. It takes a lifetime, but continuous progress in holiness is assured. Therefore, be-ware of any book or teaching that purports to teach "one sim-ple secret" of "victory" or of sanctification. There is nothing se-cret about the process. The book may indeed have something helpful to offer. But nothing—no faith, no yielding, no "letting go and letting God"—can begin the sanctifying process within you. And no secret can complete the process overnight. If you are a Christian, the process has already begun. So far as God is concerned, you are already "set apart" for his sacred service. And the Holy Spirit is eager for the process of fitting you to continue.

GOD'S WORK OR YOURS?

I just used the phrase "Let go and let God." This was a catch phrase of obscure origins from the late nineteenth century. A college student is alleged to have written on six postcards the letters L E T G O D and placed the six cards on the mantle place of his room. As a draught blew down the letter D, he is said to have discovered the secret of *letting God* control his life by *letting go* of it himself.

Many people have found the words helpful. Nevertheless, they raise a serious issue about holiness over which Christians disagree. Some see holiness as a work of God to which the Christian makes no contribution. My part as a Christian is simply to relinquish control. His part is to work through me. My efforts to strive after holiness will be unavailing. In me, that is in my flesh, dwells no good thing, so I have nothing of value to contribute. I therefore trust, that is, *I rest* in his goodness. I do not struggle to control my temper but allow Christ to handle my angry feelings. I say with Paul, "Not I but Christ." It is as though, like a sea captain, I have been up to this point at the helm of my life, and now Another is going to take over. Even faith is seen as a passivity of the will, a resting and a relaxing, not a seizing or appropriating.

I call this the *passive* view of holiness. On the other hand is the *active* view, by which Christians are called on to "wrestle and fight and pray."

Teachers of the active schools stress what they call "the means of grace." Yielding may be good but must not exclude watching and prayer, meditation on the Scriptures, fellowship with other believers, a careful effort to "maintain good works," a deliberate attempt to refrain from sin and to perform active Christian duties.

You will be puzzled as you talk to exponents of both schools to find they can give convincing and sincere testimonies to the blessings they have received as a result of practicing what seem to be conflicting principles. All schools are agreed that *faith is the key issue*. All schools are agreed that human efforts alone are unavailing and that the power for holy living must come from God. All schools are agreed that the basis of sanctification is God's intervention in the incarnation, death, resurrection and ascension of his Son, Jesus Christ, and that the help is *mediated by the Holy Spirit*, who brings about the believer's union with Christ. But given the general points of agreement, the words and phrases used become confusing and contradictory.

It need not surprise us that there should be confusion and difficulty. In the first place the New Testament itself seems to express both points of view. "Work out your own salvation with fear and trembling," writes Paul to the Philippians, apparently espousing an *active* view of the Christian life. Yet with no pause he goes on, "for [because] God is at work in you, both to will and to work for his good pleasure" (Phil 2:12-13). Now if you had only the words in the second part of the sentence, you might conclude that a Christian should lie passive in the hands of a God who is actively working. And notice. God not only makes people *do* what God wants but actually makes the decision inside them, that is, causes them to *will*.

Yet to Paul there seems to be no conflict between the first part of the sentence and the second. We are to work because God is working in us. The New Testament consistently presents both what I have called the passive and the active approaches to holiness without any sense of contradiction.

Before we look at the Scriptures, it may be as well for us to realize that we are dealing with one of the great mysteries in Scripture, the mystery of the interaction between your will and God's. The glorious work of delivering you from sin, making something altogether wonderful out of you, is a work in which both you and God have a part. Trouble arises when you start trying to map out where God's part stops and your part begins. A well-known devotional hymn describes the poet's experience of a sort of progress in sanctification. In the first verse he confesses to a time when it was, "All of self and none of Thee [God]." By the last verse, having passed through, "Some of self and some of Thee," and, "Less of self and more of Thee," he arrives at the stage where it is, "None of self and all of Thee."

I have no quarrel with the hymn. If by *self* the poet refers to his rebellious self-will, his futile struggle to do by his own resources what only God can do or his determination to reserve for himself an area of his life where God is not king, then the hymn is one all of us should sing. But it seems to me that God's working and my working need not be in competition but in harmony. I work because he works. I struggle as his Spirit within me struggles. I fight the enemy of my soul as God strives mightily in and through me. It is God's fight and yet it is my fight. And the more it is his, the more truly it is mine.

One of the key expressions of the passive teaching of sanctification is *yield*. Now in only one place in the New Testament are we urged to yield to God. In Romans 6:13-19 the expression occurs several times over. But scholars assure me that even here the word does not mean a passive lying in God's hands so much as a presenting of ourselves to be of service to God.

Is there anything passive about Paul's instruction toward the end of Romans?

Let love be genuine; hate what is evil, hold fast to what is
good; love one another with brotherly affection; outdo
one another in showing honor. Never flag in zeal, be
aglow with the Spirit, serve the Lord. Rejoice in your
hope, be patient in tribulation, be constant in prayer.
Contribute to the needs of the saints, practice hospitality.
(Rom 12:9-13)

Of course, none of us could obey these instructions apart
from the power of the Holy Spirit. But *yielding* to the Spirit consists of *obeying the Spirit's directions*, by faith and in the Spirit's
power.

How do we acquire the attributes of holy character? By waiting? Or by working? Notice the curious paradox at the beginning of Peter's second epistle. He begins by telling us that God
has "granted to us his precious and very great promises, that
through these you may escape from the corruption that is in the
world because of passion, and become partakers of the divine
nature" (2 Pet 1:4). It is all of God. And God has given us his all.

So what are we to do? Do we rest in the promises and yield
to the divine nature within? What Peter actually says is:

For this very reason *make every effort* to supplement your
faith with virtue, and virtue with knowledge, and knowledge with self-control, and self-control with steadfastness, and steadfastness with godliness, and godliness
with brotherly affection, and brotherly affection with
love. (2 Pet 1:5-7 italics added)

Use all the power at your disposal to put God's gifts to good
use!

Let there be no misunderstanding. Without God's Spirit within, our efforts are futile. No good thing could spring from our corrupt and sinful hearts. But we have been redeemed and we have been sanctified. We have been set apart for God's use. Let us then agree with God in the matter. If yielding means bowing down to him as King, let us day by day, hour by hour yield every part of our beings in allegiance to him. Let us reserve no part of our lives to serve selfish interests and ambitions. But having done that, let us assume the whole armor of God and by miraculous strength declare war on all that is evil within and without.

THE HOLY SPIRIT

People grow confused and argumentative when they talk about the Holy Spirit's role in sanctification. They may begin the discussion with warm smiles, radiating inner joy, as they testify of what he means to them. But if a difference of opinion arises, you will notice a subtle change. The smiles remain. But they freeze. Increasingly, sugary tones express more hostile words. And before long the smiles disappear altogether, and you hear words like "heresy," "gross distortions of Scriptural truth," "it seems to me you have not *the faintest* idea of the basic *principles*" and so on.

I cannot in a few sentences condense even my own limited understanding of the doctrines of the Holy Spirit, let alone explain where other views differ. But I would like to mention two simple facts which may not meet with universal approval but which could help us to understand. The old Puritans used to distinguish between what they called the *gifts*, the *operations* and the *graces* of the Holy Spirit.

In their view the gifts and the operations of the Holy Spirit had to do with God's work here on earth. By special operations through certain people and by imparting to them spiritual gifts, God brought about his sovereign will in the world. What the Puritan writers like John Owen observed was that such operations and gifts were not confined to God's servants in the Old Testament or to born-again Christians in the New. A sovereign God could by his Spirit use anyone whom he chose to.

The idea comes as a shock to twenty-first-century evangelicals who interpret "being used by God" as a reward for the virtuous and the devoted. Yet the Bible seems to support the Puritans. You will remember that on one or two occasions the disciples complained to Jesus that other people—nondisciples—were working miracles in Christ's name. Jesus warned his followers against opposing or objecting to the work. He assured them that the miracle workers did not compete with him but were on his side. Nevertheless, he warns:

> Not every one who says to me, "Lord, Lord," shall enter the kingdom of heaven, but he who does the will of my Father who is in heaven. On that day many will say to me, "Lord, Lord, did we not prophesy in your name, and cast out demons in your name, and do many mighty works in your name?" And then will I declare to them, "I never knew you; depart from me, you evildoers." (Mt 7:21-23)

It appears then that it is possible to prophesy, to exorcise demons, to perform miracles and to do these things by the Holy Spirit, yet still not to do the will of God from the heart. The test of the true servant of God, then, is not being able to perform wonders but obeying the words of the Master. This is what Jesus meant when he said, "You will know them by their fruits" (Mt 7:20).

But to return to Owen and the Puritans, the *operations* and *gifts* of the Holy Spirit were distributed to anyone as God sovereignly decided, whether they were born anew or not (1 Cor 12:11). The *graces*, in contrast, were seen only in those who were indwelt by the person of the Holy Spirit.

> And we may observe that the Holy Ghost is present with many as unto powerful operations, with whom he is not present as to gracious inhabitation; or, many are made partakers of him in his spiritual gifts, who are never made partakers of him in his saving graces.[2]

If what Owen says is true and scriptural (and I believe it is), it may explain many puzzling occurrences in our own age. Certainly it makes plain what Paul teaches in 1 Corinthians 12:31—13:3, that the fruit of the Spirit is of even greater importance than his gifts and operations. The latter may be important and should be sought, but the former alone are the true sign of his personal indwelling in the body of the believer.

The second fact I must mention deals with the filling of the Holy Spirit, necessary alike for power in service and for holiness. New Testament scholars never tire of pointing out that the command to be filled with the Spirit is just that, a *command*, that is, something you can obey. They tell us too that the words "Be . . . filled with the Holy Spirit" really mean "go on being filled continuously with the Holy Spirit." Thus the New Testament teaching (as distinct from Christ's instructions to the waiting disciples before Pentecost) is not to wait passively for something God will do to us, but to go on obeying a command. You must collaborate with the One who wishes to fill your being and, like a fountain of water, ever to spring up within you and overflow.

Two questions remain. How can you do this, how can you

obey the command to "go on being filled"? Again, what bearing had the command on holiness?

Let me try to answer the second question first. The Holy Spirit has many functions among God's people, one of which is to mold your life to conform with God's to go on sanctifying you. To the extent that your life is directed by him, to that degree the work of sanctifying you can go forward. Which brings us back to the first question: How do you "go on being filled continuously"?

How much simpler it would be if in one celestial orgasm our lives could be flooded for all time with the glory of God! But pause a moment. Spiritual ecstasy is real. You may already have experienced it. If you haven't, I hope you will—not once but many times. But it is not a process by which you forever lose control over your destiny. You may with all your heart say, "Take control of my life forever by the Holy Spirit. Let it be henceforth not my will but yours. I relinquish control from here on in."

His heart will warm as you say it. But he will not grant your request, at least not in the form you make it. If he did, he would make you less than human, a sort of spiritual automaton. What he wants is someone who moment by moment by his or her own choice goes on pleasing him. God accepts the offer we make him. The Holy Spirit will take utterly seriously the handing over of your life and body to him. But your debt is to be paid in daily, hourly installments.

Now you are in a position to understand why you must go on being filled continuously with the Holy Spirit. It means that daily, hourly you say what Christ said in Gethsemane: "Not my will, but thine be done." Was there ever anyone more filled with the Spirit than Jesus? Yet has anyone ever had to wrestle more agonizingly than he as he faced the final step in our redemption? The Spirit was leading him to the cross. The Father had sent him to die as a sin offering. By the popular understanding of what it means to be filled with the Spirit, the agonies of Gethsemane should never have occurred. Full of the Spirit he should effortlessly have brushed aside the crushing, dark horror that filled him with repugnance. He should have walked with a bright victorious smile to the cross.

But such an understanding of the Spirit's fullness is not scriptural. It reflects modern "how to live a successful life" psychologies more than godly reality. Following Jesus, we will face our lesser Gethsemanes. As we are stabbed by pain, we will be filled afresh with the Holy Spirit if we force the words from our sickened souls, "Not my will, but thine be done." To say this from the depths of our wills will cause the nausea to subside, the light to begin to show through and a trembling hope to be reawakened within us.

Not that life is to be a series of Gethsemanes. But it is to be a series of choices. And in each choice we will have the opportunity of confirming our submission to the Holy Spirit or reneging on our commitment. This is why we can only remain filled with the Spirit as we repeatedly stand by our initial commitment.

Our actions and decisions spring from attitudes of mind. They arise like waves on the sea of our thoughts, dreams and meditations. Here too continuous filling may take place.

As I sit at my desk, my eye falls on a magazine cover, depicting an earthquake scene. I am bored with the task I was doing and I am momentarily distracted by the magazine: My thoughts fly to other earthquakes I have experienced. I begin to have fantasies about them and of my own part in them.

Five minutes pass and by now my mind, by a mysterious law of its own, has passed from earthquakes to other pleasing fantasies. I catch myself and realize I am daydreaming. As I do so I suddenly remember I have not been aware of God for a couple of hours.

At this point I have two choices. The one that most appeals to me is to sigh, *Will I never learn? Is it worth the effort?* The other is to say, "Thank you for breaking through again. I'd do this all the time if it weren't for you. I praise you that the Holy Spirit is still within me. I open my mind as far as I know how to do my task for him and in the way he wants it done." This is a step in the Spirit. To go on taking steps in the Spirit is to go on being filled with the Spirit. To go on being filled with the Spirit is to grow in holiness continually.

A PASSAGE TO STUDY

Read Colossians 2:15—3:17.

1. Colossians 2:15-23. The Christians at Colossae were exposed to misguided teaching that emphasized angel worship, observation of feast days and ascetic practices. Make a list, in your own words, of acts and attitudes mentioned in the passage that are powerless to promote holiness.

2. Colossians 2:15—3:17. The passage, on the whole, promotes an *active* approach to holiness. In at least six places, however, Paul mentions *things that have already taken place*, which form the basis of an active approach. List them in your own words. If you can understand what they mean, kneel and by faith give God thanks that they are true.

3. Make a list of things Paul tells you to *do*. If you are working

with the King James Version, check with another translation for such words as *mortify*. Consider to what extent you can put into practice the instructions he gives.

Note. "The old man"—you as you were without Christ; "the new man"—your new identity in Christ.

10

Deliverance from Drudgery

Mia gave us a teapot.

Mia is a woman who has a knack of winning the confidence of teenage kids in trouble. She is also observant and thoughtful. Two things about the teapot struck me. First, it was beautiful—unglazed, dull red, exquisite in shape and overlaid with ceramic flowers. The other thing I noticed is that she had spotted an empty niche near our fireplace that was waiting for something like that teapot. Her choice was a hand-and-glove fit. Mia proudly told us, "It's unique. The craftsman only made one like this."

A week later the Changs came over for coffee and Dr. Chang spotted the teapot. "Why I do believe . . ." he began as he crossed the room toward it. "Yes, it is. These used to be made in a village near where I was born. The earth there . . . it's different from anywhere else." There was growing excitement in his voice. "I remember exactly how they made them." He paused and his wife leaned over and spotted Chinese characters on the inner surface. "They're very rare," he said. "Even in China."

CRAFTSMANSHIP, TECHNOLOGY
AND CRAMMING FOR EXAMS

Craftsmanship. It has little place in our technology dominated world. I have three handsome plastic plant pots, all identical and from the same mold. I bought them because I liked them. What do I care if five thousand others were manufactured? Mine are still beautiful. The curse of technology does not lie in its capacity to multiply beauty but in its ruthless suppression of creativity. It is not what it does to things that matters, but what it does to people. The workers who pulled my plant pots off the assembly line probably felt nothing at all as they did so. But the person who made the teapot must have been proud and satisfied.

I am intrigued by the relationship between work and drudgery. Mia's teapot was obviously a labor of love. Its beauty witnesses eloquently to the joy someone had in making it. It is true that technology has made factory work drudgery. A visit to an auto factory has convinced me of this. Yet drudgery existed before technology so that we cannot lay all the blame on mass production.

Sometimes when I mow the lawn I enjoy myself. The sky may be clear, the mosquitoes few, the air fresh and my mind carefree. In spite of the din of the motor, I enjoy the wind on my skin and hear it rushing through the trees. When the job is done, satisfaction kindles warmly inside me as I look at the smooth sweep of green. Yet there are days when I resent the job and do it with ill grace. Why the difference?

Working with others helps. With two or three of the family

working together it's a lot more fun. The labor is halved and the satisfaction doubled. We find ourselves on better terms afterward as we put equipment away in the garden shed. I am reminded of the black women I have often watched in the Caribbean. They sing in chorus as they weave their colorful baskets, purses and hats, threading the straw and raffia with nimble fingers.

Yet it can't be just company. Company alleviates drudgery. Slaves sang together in cotton fields and sugar cane plantations. The singing helped but drudgery was drudgery.

I think the women weaving flowered baskets enjoyed what they did whether they were together or not. At least they said they did when I asked them. They seemed proud of their work. They had the satisfaction of seeing beauty grow from their fingers. Is this then the difference between work and drudgery, the feeling of satisfaction and pride in a job well done?

Does it matter how beautiful the thing you make is? I know it helps to admire your ceramic or your weaving or your lawn. But people in days gone by performed jobs we called drudgery and got the same quality of pride as my Chinese craftsman or the Caribbean basket weavers.

Take a scrubbed wooden floor for instance. Drudgery? I've known women smile happily as the whitened boards shine clean again. Not all women, I grant you, but for some it was therapy. They would look at the newly dried floor as though they loved it. They were proud of their strength and their thoroughness, and contemptuous about the sloppy job other women did. The same holds true for other chores like polishing silver, making feather pillows, plowing a straight furrow or even cutting down a tree. And as the author *of Zen and the Art of Mo-*

torcycle Maintenance points out, there can even be satisfaction in tuning a motor bike engine.

The subject is important for the happiness and even the holiness of us all. To one Christian student study is drudgery and cramming for a test a nightmare. To others it is—if not fun—at least something they feel good about accomplishing. Since most of us will spend many working hours "earning our living" in some office, school, factory or kitchen, it would be wise to ask ourselves how we may solve the problem of drudgery and whether it is possible to learn the art of fulfillment in our work.

Let me begin with study. Many students come to me complaining of tiredness and laziness. "I just don't seem to be able to get down to work," they tell me. "Then when exams come I panic." It seems to make no difference whether the student gets straight A's or just gets by. The problem is the same: Uncompleted assignments, essays not handed in, revulsion against boring texts, anxiety and feverish last-minute cramming. Some students ask me for certificates to say that they are emotionally unwell.

While some subjects may appeal to us more than others, I believe any subject, even the most unappealing, would interest us if it were taught by someone who loved it and could infect us with his love. But authors of textbooks often obfuscate and dishearten us. They take the colors from the material and insist on black and various shades of gray. Or their verbal gardens are overgrown with weeds and their forests choked with such a dense undergrowth that we are obliged to hack our way forward, machete in hand, longing for the sight of the sun.

But when we have made due allowance for impossible texts and dreary lecturers, there remains much to be said about the

obstacles to progress that are in ourselves. We are tyrannized by
our conceited expectations and, failing to meet them, are lashed
by unrealistic self-recriminations. Some of us are immature and
react to academic work much as we did when as children we
were sent to restore order in the chaos of our littered bedrooms.
We are rebellious children who, in psychological jargon, "lack
motivation" to study because we respond to our professors as
we would to parents. Or else we are fearful, imagining ourselves
alone in the struggle for understanding, not realizing that many
students around us are playing various forms of academic one-
upmanship to hide their own fears.

And forever ahead of us lie the frightening rituals we go
through in examination halls. The silences. The rustling paper.
The measured tread of the invigilator, the proctor. Frantic scrib-
blings. The merciless moving of the fingers on the clock. The increasing oppression of stale cigarette smoke. An inevitable smart
aleck who hands the paper in before the period is half over.

We put the horror away in the back of our minds, telling ourselves it isn't so bad as all that. Yet our brains freeze over as the
time approaches, and our notes stare back at us blankly and
meaninglessly.

Changes in examination policies have not alleviated the
problem. Pass-Fail grading systems, peer evaluation and other
methods seem not to get to the root of the student's difficulty.

I remember the relief I felt when I quit worrying about exams. I was studying human pathology at the time. I recall the
desk I was sitting at and the view of tree tops from my open,
leaded windows. With half my mind I was reading and with the
other half I was worrying about such questions as, *Am I really
absorbing this stuff? Is it likely to come up in an exam? Maybe this*

textbook is too detailed. Am I going too slowly? Should I get another textbook? Ought I to rely on lecture notes? Why is it so boring?

From somewhere the thought came: *Why not read this chapter as unto the Lord?*

Not worry about exams? I caught my breath. One part of me knew that I would experience relief and enjoy my work more. Another part of me rebelled. The suggestion seemed dangerous. My examiners were not interested in godly conscientiousness but in my covering the material.

The struggle was brief and I opted for godliness. I was sick of the drudgery of studying for grades and of the pervasive anxiety that inhibited real study. I had already grasped the kind of study principles that "how to study" books describe so that my change of orientation entailed no change of method. Indeed I became more methodical. But the pressure left me. "For you Lord," became my motivation. To my joy I found his yoke easy and his burden light so that I studied with rest in my soul. Pathology grew more interesting. I could afford to be curious about what I was reading. I took pride in writing brief outlines of chapters I read through. The drudgery melted away and a sense of satisfaction and gratitude took its place. Exams or no exams, I would study for God. And I took time off to play tennis with a carefree spirit.

I don't mean that I forgot I had a certain number of months to complete a course. But my sense of responsibility had changed. I was no longer responsible *to pass the examination.* Rather I was responsible to use my study time in a way that pleased God. I covered the same ground but was carefree and enjoyed what I was doing. I certainly learned a lot more though how this affected my marks I do not know. Nor do I care. I was no longer working for grades but for Christ. Study had become for me what making the teapot had been for the old Chinese. I drew satisfaction from the activity and from the end result of a chapter grasped as well as my abilities allowed.

Of course I would slip back from time to time. Pleasing Christ in my studies was like learning a new swimming stroke. It had to be practiced. Yet my studies were never again the same.

I hear someone asking me, "What do I do when the course material turns me off completely? I've done all I can to change my attitude, but my mind just doesn't work. Is it my Christian duty to plough through stuff I have no hope of grasping?" Of course not. Consult someone—your instructor or a guidance counselor. If you are taking a course that you have no ability for, perhaps you should consider withdrawing from it as soon as possible. Christ's yoke is easy and his burden light. He wants to teach you *joy* in learning. He has given you certain natural gifts, but he has not made you an all-round genius.

EASY AND LIGHT

I must be careful not to leave you with the wrong impression. When Christ talked about giving his followers a light burden, he was not promising them an absence of work. From the beginning of this chapter we have really been discussing the difference between work and drudgery. Heavy work can be tiring but deeply satisfying. Toil and drudgery imply enslavement of some kind and have to do with revulsion. Nowhere does the Bible encourage laziness.

I have been avoiding the theological issues and have been talking more about the psychology of work. Let me make a start by quoting verses. "Whatever your hand finds to do, do it with your might," says the writer of Ecclesiastes (Eccles 9:10). Paul writes:

> Slaves, obey your earthly masters with fear and trembling, single-mindedly, as serving Christ. Do not offer merely the outward show of service, to curry favour with men, but, as slaves of Christ, do whole-heartedly the will of God. Give the cheerful service of those who serve the Lord, not men. For you know that whatever good each man may do, slave or free, will be repaid him by the Lord. (Eph 6:5-8 NEB)

You could be misled by a red herring at this point. Paul was not justifying slavery when he wrote these words. They apply to employed free men as well as to slaves: to students, factory and office workers alike. Rather he gives us the spirit, quality and motivation that should characterize all work done by Christians, anywhere and under any circumstances.

Let me in a very simple way try to explain what work and drudgery are all about. Christians are people who have been set free to enjoy working. Humans were made to work. Before Adam fell, he was given farming, supervisory and scientific tasks. He was to govern the created order, to name and classify vegetable and animal life (Gen 2:15-20). With disobedience and the Fall came a change in his relationship with work. "Accursed shall be the ground on your account," God told him. "With labour you shall win your food from it all the days of your life. . . . You shall gain your bread by the sweat of your brow until you return to the ground; for from it you were taken" (Gen 3:17-19 NEB).

From that time no one has been free from toil, unless he or she was powerful enough to make others do the work. But with redemption a change came. The redeemed man or woman is freed from the *tyranny of necessity*. Christians are to cease from care about food and shelter and to trust a heavenly Father. Anxiety must deliberately be laid on one side. They may work as hard as ever, but the ache has gone from the drudgery. The ground may still be cursed, but redeemed people have been freed. They may discover the joy of working for love of God. And the harder they work, the more their soul exults.

Notice, however, we are not back in Eden. A glance around us will quickly remove any hopes we may entertain about that. Technology has merely changed the form by which the ground exerts its curse on humankind. Those who once sweat with aching back behind a heavy plow now stands beside a conveyer belt and tightens a million identical nuts with a power tool. Their bodies may have grown soft, but their minds are weary with the weight of emptiness.

I cannot tell you all you should do if you work on a conveyer belt. I do say: Tighten nuts for Christ, not for the foreman. But I also say: Ask God whether there is a job more fitting for a redeemed person. He may show you one. On the other hand you may prefer to stick around Detroit tightening nuts because it pays more. In that case you will be a slave to Mammon.

THE SECULAR AND THE PROFANE

Some men and women are called from their studies or their jobs to serve God in another way. Peter and John were called from catching fish to catching persons. Matthew was called from his position with the income tax department to become a Christian worker.

On the face of it, nothing could be more important than winning souls and fitting them for glory. It is only natural, then, that we should sometimes wonder whether we are wasting our time in our studies or jobs. Who would lick stamps if they could win souls? Who would study applied math rather than "be involved in meaningful interpersonal relationships"?

Unfortunately we oversimplify the issues. For one thing our motives get in the way. It is just as possible to run away *to* the mission field to escape difficulties at home as it is to avoid the mission field because I am too comfortable where I am. To add to our confusion we may be pressured by the faculty (to get another degree), by parents and industry (to get a good job) and by Christian workers (to be a "full-timer").

Several paragraphs back I quote extensively from Pauline epistles where servants are urged to do the job they are doing with all they've got. The New Testament contains many similar exhortations to people in all walks of life. *No where, in any part of the New Testament, is there any word of general exhortation urging Christians to consider leaving their everyday tasks for full-time work.* To face sacrifice? Yes. To count all things but loss? Yes. But if the divine commission to evangelize the world was primarily a call that Christians should leave *inferior* occupations and become professional evangelists, the idea occurred to none of the New Testament writers. It would seem rather that those whose call it was so to "leave their nets" were to be as divinely gifted for their task as they were divinely called.

Please do not misinterpret my remarks. I am not belittling evangelistic endeavor or full-time service. My point is that it is nowhere reflected in the New Testament as being an activity of superior quality. What matters with God is that wherever you are and whatever you do, you act always and only for the glory of God. If you seek anything, you must "seek after the best gifts," not the most "spiritual" jobs. Until such gifts are imparted, the best preparation for the service of God is to serve him in what you have to do *right now*.

WITNESS THROUGH SUCCESS?

Let me return to the issue of doing whatever comes to your hand with all your might. It has been suggested that the Christian who so works automatically serves as a witness to his Lord. Certainly the attitude awakens people's curiosity and invites comment.

But there is a subtle distortion of this truth that pervades Western Christianity. The idea seems to be that *success is what convinces*. If only a Christian student can get straight A's, then his testimony will count. One shines for Jesus from the top of the tree. The top athlete packs a powerful punch for the Savior; the successful Christian billionaire convinces unconverted millionaires that Jesus is real and powerful.

Powerful to do what? To make us all straight A students? By such a standard most followers of Jesus are failures and will forever remain so. The widow who casts her two mites into the offering would get nowhere in today's Christian hierarchy.

Let me encourage you, then, not to think primarily of success. Should God grant it to you, rejoice and praise him. Your aim is not "success" in the way the world around you measures success but to please Christ by the way you tackle even unrewarding tasks. Work is not your steppingstone to "higher things." It is an act of worship to a Savior.

There is a story of a monastery where the monks sang God's praises fervently and joyfully, but tunelessly and discordantly.

By the time their voices reached God's throne, however, the joy and the fervor had transmuted the sounds into a majestic paean of music.

The same sort of thing can happen to your work. However mean the task, perform it as an act of praise to God. It is recorded of Brother Lawrence, a seventeenth-century lay brother, "that he was well pleased when he could take up a straw from the ground for the love of God, seeking Him only, and nothing else, nor even His gifts." Because of his clumsiness and general stupidity, Brother Lawrence was obliged to work in the kitchen of the monastery, a work for which he had a natural aversion. But we read, "having accustomed himself to do everything there for the love of God, and with prayer upon all occasions for His grace to do his work well, he had found everything easy during the fifteen years he had been employed there." For Lawrence, every action was an act of worship.

It is significant that work so done becomes lighter, less burdensome. Yet it is not for that reason I recommend it. I recommend it because *God is worthy of praise* and work is a misspent opportunity when it is anything less than worship.

> Fill Thou my life, O Lord my God,
> In every part with praise,
> That my whole being may proclaim
> Thy being and Thy ways.
>
> Not for the lip of praise alone,
> Nor e'en the praising heart,
> I ask, but for a life made up
> Of praise in every part.

Praise in the common things of life,
Its going out and in;
Praise in each duty and each deed,
However small and mean.[1]

So you need never envy people around you who seem more talented than you. Your business is not to excel them, to covet their brains or gifts, but to give your own abilities to your Lord in worship.

ORGANIZING YOUR TIME

Discipline is important. Many students fritter away their time in endless coffee table discussions. Christian committee meetings consume unnecessarily large chunks of time. Meetings and Bible studies, important as they are, can serve as an escape from less attractive duties.

Do you organize your time? Do you map out your week's program? On paper? It's a good exercise, so long as you are realistic and don't overload yourself. Write down how you would *like* to spend your time. The result may shock you if you have never tried it before. You may discover that time cannot stretch to include all you hoped to do. It will make you face where your true priorities lie.

Hopefully it will also help you to be truthful with yourself. Don't cut out time for recreation or for socializing. Allow yourself a little extra time at meals to chat with friends. A life devoted to Christ is not an unremitting nose-to-the grindstone life. The real waste of time comes from meaningless conversations, escapist reading, TV watching or from sitting through long committee meetings sloppily run. Have the courage to walk out of a committee meeting with, "Please excuse me, Mr. Chairman, I have to leave now." Then get up and go. If the chairman protests, smile and say, "I'm sorry, but you'll have to manage without me." When held hypnotically by TV, deliberately break your trance, wash your face in cold water and get back to your books.

LOAVES AND FISHES

My sympathies go out to the student or office worker whose talents are mediocre. I don't know why God didn't make you a genius. And though you may not believe me, the brightest people suffer the same problem as you do. They are rarely satisfied with what they've got and are usually conscious of people brighter than themselves.

It matters not how much you've got but what you do with it. Use your mediocre gifts for God. Give him your life and with it your brain and your gifts, such as they are. Give him your energy, your time and your strength.

Twenty centuries ago a crowd of five thousand people were hungry after a day of listening to Jesus. The disciples were nonplussed when Christ suggested they feed the crowd. Close at hand was a boy with five barley loaves and two fish, and, as Philip, stating the obvious, pointed out, "What are they among so many?" Yet given to Jesus, the mediocre offering fed multitudes.

You are a poor student? An average worker? Your abilities are below par? Don't bury them. Don't hide them under a bushel. Give them to the Savior. He calls you to study for him, to work for him with all the strength you possess. He is not concerned with what this world calls success. He did not draw you to himself because you had superior potential but because he wanted to share joy with you. Give him your loaves and fishes. Give them to him freely. No miracle may take place. But his heart will be gladdened and you will begin to taste the joy of work well done and to escape the chains of drudgery.

A PASSAGE TO STUDY

Read Genesis 1:26-30; 2:15-20; 3:16-19.

Paradise is popularly conceived of as a state of pleasure without labor, where one enjoys the bounty of creation freely and effortlessly.

1. Make a list of the activities humans were expected to carry out before the Fall. To what extent do these reflect God's image in man?

2. What change occurs in human work as a result of the Fall?

11

The Fight

Soldiers of Christ, arise,
And put your armour on;
Strong in the strength which God supplies
Through His eternal Son;
Strong in the Lord of hosts,
And in His mighty power;
Who in the strength of Jesus trusts
Is more than conqueror.[1]

We think of war as ugly—and so it is. Throughout history no war has been fought without terror, barbarity, cruelty, the agony of the dying and the hopeless sobbing of enslaved and bereaved men, women and children. Modern warfare with its potential for indiscriminate mass destruction has assumed an unreal, nightmare quality. We do well to pray and to work for peace on earth.

Yet in our modern revulsion against war we are inclined to forget that the same wars that gave rise to atrocities and barbarism also produced the noblest and best in humanity. I would not justify war, yet what I say is a fact. Unnatural courage, unbelievable self-sacrifice, devotion, loyalty and love, resourcefulness in the face of impossible odds, endurance beyond the limits of human strength: these too are part of the picture.

Such things become the themes of poetry, song and legend. And though we may regret that the songs perpetuate the myth of the glory of war, we must not forget that just as lilies bloom white in cesspools so human virtues have reached unparalleled beauty amid the horrors of war.

The New Testament condemns the spirit of war. "What causes wars, and what causes fighting's among you?" asks James the brother of our Lord. "Is it not your passions that are at war in your members? You desire and do not have; so you kill. And you covet and cannot obtain; so you fight and wage war" (Jas 4:1-2).

Yet it need not surprise us that as an image to convey the nature of Christian living, the Holy Spirit uses that of warfare. No image could be more apt. The same courage, the same watchfulness, loyalty, endurance, resourcefulness, strength, skill, knowledge of the enemy, the same undying resolve to fight to the end come what may and at whatever cost *must* characterize Christian living as they do earthly warfare.

But I am expressing it the wrong way. War is not something that illustrates aspects of Christian living. Christian living is war. Indeed I would go further. Earthly warfare is not the real warfare. It is but a faint, ugly reflection of the real thing. It is into the *real* war that the Christian is to plunge. Wars on earth are but tremors felt from an earthquake light-years away. The Christian's war takes place at the epicenter of the earthquake. It is infinitely more deadly, while the issues that hang on it make earth's most momentous questions no more than village gossip.

Are you then prepared to follow Christ into the deadliest and most fundamental of all wars? It is imperative that you size the matter up. Warfare costs. The dangers and trials are real. Don't act impulsively on a wave of momentary enthusiasm, but think what you are doing. Count the cost.

Yet in saying, "Count the cost," what am I saying? Am I suggesting that it is possible to live as a Christian without warfare? For this is not true. The real counting should have been done before you became a Christian. *To acknowledge Jesus as Savior and Lord is to join an army. Whether you know it or not, you have enlisted.* The only other option open to you is to become a deserter, to hide your uniform and pretend you are someone whom you are not. Now to be a deserter is not to *leave* the army (celestial regulations make no provision for the discharge of personnel) but to evade your responsibility to your commanding officer.

> Am I a soldier of the cross,
> A follower of the Lamb,
> And shall I fear to own His cause,
> Or blush to speak His name?
>
> In the name, the precious name
> Of Him who died for me,
> I'll fight to win the promised crown
> What're my cross may be.[2]

I do not retract my suggestion that you count the cost. I only say, Read on. Let me make clear to you the nature of the battle you are to be engaged in, the enemies you fight, the weapons

you must use and the manner by which you may fight victori-
ously. For your choice lies between fighting and fleeing, between loyalty and desertion. Therefore I say, Look well at what
you may anticipate and at what is expected of you.

The old Puritans used to speak of three fronts from which
Christ's soldier may expect attack: the world, the flesh and the
devil. To these the New Testament adds a fourth: death. We have
partly looked at them already, but let me explain what is meant
by all four.

THE BATTLE WITH THE WORLD

The Bible speaks of the world in three ways. There is *the planet
earth*. "The earth is the LORD's and the fullness thereof, the world
and those who dwell therein" (Ps 24:1). Then there is *the world
of humans*, the world God loves and for which Christ died. "For
God so loved the world that he gave his only son . . ." (Jn 3:16).
Finally there is *the spirit of the age*. "Do not love the world,"
writes John, "or the things in the world. If any one loves the
world, love for the Father is not in him" (1 Jn 2:15). He is referring to the age we live in, its values, its goals, its lifestyle.

Which world, then, are we to fight? Clearly we must look
hard at what I have called the spirit of the age. Yet is there any
sense in which we will find ourselves in conflict with the world
of humans, the world for which Jesus died? In any case, how are
we to define the spirit of the age? What is there about it that we
fight? Do we fight to bring about a new political order? Are we
to attempt to replace the present government with godly government, to bring about a Cromwell-style revolution?

In John's mind is no such thought. "For all that is in the
world," he continues, "the lust of the flesh and the lust of the

eyes and the pride of life, is not of the Father but is of the world" (1 Jn 2:16). Three lusts: flesh, eyes and pride.

Lust is desire made into a god. I eat when I am hungry. I even eat my favorite foods when I get a chance. But if I were to live to eat, to make a principal goal in my life of the pleasures of an epicurean palate, then you could accuse me of fleshly lust for food. And as C. S. Lewis points out, to lust for food does not mean merely to overeat. It can equally well manifest itself in the spirit of the dilettante who discriminates against any food that offends the susceptibilities of his finely tuned palate. In the same way any bodily appetite for sleep, for physical recreation or for sex becomes a bodily lust at the point where to satisfy them interferes in the smallest degree with serving and glorifying Christ.

Already I have dealt in a previous chapter with the spirit of worldliness (the lust of the flesh, the lust of the eye and the pride of life). The battle with "the world" and with "the devil" are at this point one and the same battle, and in the section on satanic temptation I have suggested how you should fight it.

But worldliness is more than a way of looking at things, more than making physical pleasures, beautiful material possessions and pride into gods that we worship. As a Christian you are surrounded by worldly people, people who live for advancement, for material gain or for all of these. To the extent that you renounce the spirit of the age you live in and make Christ supreme, your lifestyle will clash with theirs. Some of them will resent you. You may experience petty barbs or humiliating rejection. "In the world," said Jesus, "you have tribulation; but be of good cheer, I have overcome the world" (Jn 16:33).

There has been much misunderstanding about the Christian's relationship with the world. Some Christians in every age have withdrawn totally from contact with non-Christian people. Monasteries and ruined abbeys remain as monuments to their beliefs. In modern evangelical circles we withdraw by minimizing our contact with unbelievers and relating only to believers. We rely for our social life upon church-related activities, and for our entertainment on pretty cathode-ray tubes. We have confused separation from sin with isolation from sinners.

But Jesus does not call us to isolation. True, we must not be *of* the world (not share its values) but be *in* it. To withdraw from it is to "hide our light under a bushel" or to be "the salt of the earth" sealed in plastic packages. It is also to avoid the pain of conflict and rejection. To avoid social contact with non-Christian people is to retire within the walls of the church's battlements. It is to change the militant church into a besieged church—a change the devil very much wants to bring about.

Two things, then, are apparent about our battle with the world. We are to hate, detest and renounce its spirit. We are to tear from within our bosoms any treacherous tendency to worship food, sleep, sex, beautiful possessions and reputation. All those things, while legitimate in their place, must never become objects of worship. We cannot defeat them by becoming ascetics. Only by allowing Jesus to be Lord can we win the battle. Whenever conflict arises between obeying Christ and giving way to an otherwise legitimate desire, Christ must come first.

For example I have a silly fear that I won't get enough rest when I serve God. Clearly I must be sensible and allow myself proper rest and recreation. But sometimes the matter of sleep becomes so important that I get scared. In my fear I blot out every other consideration. "Unless I insist on rest *now*, I'm not going to be able to cope later." Fear threatens to overwhelm faith. Only when I adopt the attitude of a soldier, only when I quit worrying about consequences and obey orders is my fear allayed and my peace restored. Sure I get weary! But who doesn't in wartime? "Share in suffering," Paul writes to Timothy, "as a good soldier of Christ Jesus" (2 Tim 2:3).

Being in the world, then, interacting daily with our fellow humans, it is inevitable that some disagreeable consequences will follow. "Many are the afflictions of the righteous," warns the psalmist (Ps 34:19). Jewish Christians were reminded that in their early Christian experience they endured

> the challenge of great suffering and held firm. Some of
> you were abused and tormented to make a public show,
> while others stood loyally by those who were so treated.
> For indeed you shared the sufferings of the prisoners, and
> you cheerfully accepted the seizure of your possessions.
> (Heb 10:32-34 NEB)

Their persecution did not arise from their self-righteousness or their obnoxious conduct but simply because of their loyalty to Christ. And while we live in a more tolerant day, we must expect, as soldiers of Christ, that some form of hardship will follow prompt obedience of orders. We must also be aware that it is now late in the afternoon of the day of tolerance and that as darkness falls, the hardships and dangers will increase terrifyingly. Therefore, while like Christ we must love the world of people, it will rise against us eventually as it rose against him and tried to destroy him.

THE BATTLE AGAINST THE FLESH

When Paul uses the word *flesh*, he is often not talking about our bodily desires but about the habits, instincts and tendencies of mind as well as of body that we retain from the time before we met Christ. In the chapter on holiness I pointed out that in dealing with these old patterns of mind, there is no conflict between yielding to the Holy Spirit and taking other active steps to overcome them. Here again an unceasing warfare is to be maintained. Says Paul, "I perceive that there is in my bodily members a different law, fighting against the law that my reason approves and making me a prisoner" (Rom 7:23 NEB). Peter himself talks about "passions of the flesh that wage war against your soul" (1 Pet 2:11).

Other aspects of the war might scare us, but this aspect more than any other discourages and disheartens us. And since morale is vital to victory, discouragement is deadly. Read again the section in the chapter on holiness that deals with the relation between peace and holiness. Read the section in "His Infernal Majesty" on Satan the accuser. Of course you may get wounded in battle! Of course you may get knocked off your feet! But it is the man or woman who gets up and fights again that is a true warrior. What would you think of a soldier who in the midst of battle sat down and said, "I'm no good. It's no use trying any more. Nothing seems to work"?

There is no place for giving up. The warfare is so much bigger than our personal humiliations. To feel sorry for oneself is totally inappropriate. Over such a soldier I would pour a bucket of icy water. I would drag him to his feet, kick him in the rear end and put his sword in his hand and shout, "Now fight!" In some circumstances one must be cruel to be kind.

What if you have fallen for a tempting ruse of the enemy? What if you're not the most brilliant swordsman in the army? You hold Excalibur in your hand! Get behind the lines for a break if you're too weak to go on, and strengthen yourself with a powerful draught of the wine of Romans 8:1-4. Then get back into the fight before your muscles get stiff!

But watch. Nothing is more important in your battle with the flesh than to be alert. Once you start to grow careless and cocky—watch out! "Let any one who thinks that he stands take heed lest he fall" (1 Cor 10:12). For if you cannot afford to give way to discouragement, you can afford even less to be too sure of yourself. Cockiness and discouragement are two sides of the same coin of conceit. Get rid of it. You're no good—be proud of *that*. You're a nobody whom God has made a prince of heaven. Rejoice in a God who recruits bums and equips them as soldiers of a King.

THE BATTLE AGAINST THE POWERS OF DARKNESS

"For we are not contending against flesh and blood [other men and women], but against the principalities, against the powers" (Eph 6:12). In the passage in Ephesians 6, Paul concludes by urging us to pray "on every occasion in the power of the Spirit. To this end keep watch and persevere, always interceding for all God's people" (Eph 6:18 NEB).

> Hell's legions are terrified of prayer.
> Satan trembles when he sees
> The weakest saint upon his knees.

Hell was so fearful of Daniel's resolve to pray that we read of all-out attack in the heavenlies on his prayer. An angelic visitor told the trembling prophet:

Do not be afraid, Daniel, for from the first day that you set your heart on understanding this and on humbling yourself before your God, your words were heard, and I have come in response to your words. But the prince of the kingdom of Persia was withstanding me for twenty-one days; then behold, Michael, one of the chief princes, came to help me, for I had been left there with the kings of Persia. (Dan 10:12-13 NASB)

Human prayers and battles in celestial places!

In a dramatic scene in Revelation 8, an angel before the throne of God took incense mingled with the prayers of believing Christians and threw them on the altar before the throne. Smoke rose up from incense-sweetened prayers, encircling the rulers of the universe.

But from the same altar the angel took the same hot coals on which the prayers had been thrown and flung them from heaven to earth. As they fell, we read, "And there were peals of thunder, voices, flashes of lightning, and an earthquake" (Rev 8:5). Such is the explosive might of prayer.

In the chapter on prayer I mentioned many things that can help you in praying. But there is one specific item in the New Testament that relates to prayer and the battle with the powers of darkness. When you know of a brother or sister who has been alienated from Christian fellowship because of personal failure, be quick to forgive and restore such a one to fellowship. It is in this context that Paul writes, "For Satan must not be allowed to get the better of us; we know his wiles all too well" (2 Cor 2:11 NEB). Do not let your prayers be hindered by disagreements, self-righteousness, unforgiveness.

THE SPIRIT AND THE BATTLE

Some remarks I have made may make it sound as though our fight is a defensive one. Let me quickly change any such impression.

At the heart of the matter is the principle, "The battle is the LORD's" (1 Sam 17:47). How many battles have been won because of the genius of a leader. Alexander, Julius Caesar, Napoleon, Nelson, Alexander, Patton—how their names stir us! The whole of Scripture makes it plain to us that the battle is not our personal battle. It is part of a war. We are led by the Unconquerable One. And good general that he is, he knows his soldiers by name and concerns himself with their safety and well being. There is to be no cannon fodder among heaven's soldiers. The issue of the battle rests entirely on the unconquerable might of our Leader.

Indeed we fight in a war that is already won. It was won when Jesus burst from a sealed tomb. In World War II when the allies invaded Europe, the whole world knew that the war was really over. Months of death and bitter fighting lay ahead. There would be cold and exhaustion, peril and pain, the crumple of bombs and the sickening death swoops of flaming aircraft. But the end had really come. No one, except perhaps for an insane führer, was in any doubt as to that fact. The curtain was falling. The grim show was finished.

We are now in precisely the same position. The last invasion is on. "In the world," stated Jesus, "you have tribulation, but be of good cheer, I *have* overcome the world" (Jn 16:33 italics added). "Thanks be to God," Paul shouts in exultation, "who gives us the victory through our Lord Jesus Christ" (1 Cor 15:57). Or again, "Thanks be to God, who in Christ always leads us in triumph" (2 Cor 2:14).

Now there are times when you will feel anything but like a member *of* a triumphant army. You will feel alone, small, weak. The battle therefore is also essentially a battle of *faith.* When wracked with fear and doubt, it is "the victory that overcometh the world, *even our faith*" (1 Jn 5:4 KJV, italics added). Or as the New English Bible puts it, "Every child *of* God is victor over the godless world. The victory that defeats the world *is our faith*, for who is victor over the world but he who believes that Jesus is the Son of God?" (1 Jn 5:4-5).

It is therefore essential, mop-up operation or no, that we fight effectively. "Fight the good fight of faith," Paul urges his young protégé, Timothy (1 Tim 6:12 KJV).

"Through faith," says the author of the Hebrews' letter, "they overthrew kingdoms, established justice, saw God's promises fulfilled. They muzzled ravening lions, quenched the fury of fire, escaped death by the sword. Their weakness was turned into strength, they grew powerful in war, they put foreign armies to rout" (Heb 11:33-34 NEB).

No. We cannot sit back on our haunches. The moments before victory can see the fighting wax the fiercest. So Paul is careful about the way he fights. "I am like a boxer who does not beat the air," he tells us. "I bruise my own body and make it know its master" (1 Cor 9:26-27 NEB). In 2 Timothy he warns, "Take your share of hardship, like a good soldier of Christ Jesus. A soldier on active service will not let himself be involved in civilian affairs; he must be wholly at his commanding officer's disposal" (2 Tim 2:3-4 NEB).

Wholly at his commanding officer's disposal. The words take my breath away. Am I entangled with "civilian affairs"? Do the "cares of this life spring up and choke the word"? Or am *I entirely at the disposal* of my Commanding Officer? The hour of victory is no time to fritter life away on trifles.

The last battle is on. There will be no more battles when this one is won. You will have no opportunity after this life to march with a victorious army in the steps of the Conqueror of time and eternity.

THE LAST ENEMY

To talk about death is the "in" thing these days. Psychiatrists, physicians, nurses, social workers, pastoral counselors all attend lectures and read books on the psychology of dying. The dying patient was once surrounded by false smiles of reassurance (and whispered behind-the-bedscreen conferences) sometimes utterly alone as his or her nearest and dearest played a cheerful "let's pretend" game. Somehow the patient knew he or she had to act the false part and pretend along with the rest. Now the patient is bluntly informed that he or she has two to four weeks to put things in order.

Some men and women let the words float over their heads. The shock is too great. Reality melts into unreality, and false hope, the friend of the weak, comes to their rescue. To others the blow is shattering. They struggle to their knees, then slowly stand again, sickened and weak and hopeless. I remember a Christian colleague who knew he was dying and who said to me, "Yes, I guess I've accepted it now." But his eyes were downcast and his shoulders wearily slumped. There was no joy. We could not reach each other for he seemed already beyond death, sitting up in bed and talking to me from a distance of light-years.

Yet I have the warmest and happiest memories of a middle-aged nurse dying of leukemia. She named the precise diagnosis accurately with a smile almost of mischief on her face. "So how'd you feel?" I asked.

"You know as well as I do," she was looking me in the eye: "It'll be anything from three to six months. I feel better after the transfusions. I'll have energy to do quite a few things."

"Like what?"

"I've always wanted to learn to play the piano but never got down to it. Just enough to play one or two hymns. We've bought a piano and I'm going to start next week. I'll enjoy the kids too. I won't need to work so I can spend more time with them. And," her eyes kindled, "I think we'll be able to manage a little trip, my husband and I, before I die."

I wanted to laugh and cry at the same time.

"What about your husband?"

Her eyes clouded for a moment.

"I don't know. It's he who worries me most. Will he be scared to touch me? To make love? I don't want him to feel afraid of me. Besides . . ." she looked away. I held her hand.

"It's so good of you to come and see me. I just wanted to talk."

And talk she did. Happily, realistically, wistfully, humorously. It had been a good life, she told me. Her heart flowed with gratitude to God. She was determined to extract from the last few weeks whatever God had to offer her here. For her the last enemy was thoroughly defeated.

I know an old lady who shares the same triumph. "Don't let them stick tubes in me and try to make me live on," she begged me once. "God's been so good to me, and I'm happier now than I've ever been. I have so many things to enjoy here. But I'm ready to leave too. In fact . . . it will be nice to be with him forever. So promise me you won't let them." I promised.

Sometimes I grow frustrated with Thomas à Kempis (*The Imitation of Christ*). He is on the ball in so many ways, yet at other times he misses the point completely. However his chapter on death is superb. "Think daily upon thine own death," he tells us. Look your enemy in the eye. Can you?

John Donne devoted a whole book to the contemplation of death (*Devotions*). Its complex yet beautiful sentences held me spellbound and changed my life. John Donne so grappled with and triumphed over death that when his own death came, he arranged his shroud carefully, lay down with composure, crossed his hands prayerfully across his chest and, rejoicing and peaceful, died.

This book is not the place for me to discuss the doctrine of death. You must know already that the believer's hope springs from a Christ who has so conquered death that his followers, like him, will pass physically through the portals of death, to be raised, physically, beyond them. Read the chapter on the resurrection in John Stott's *Basic Christianity* if you want to get a better grasp of the doctrine.

Rather, it is with *the fear* of death that I want to deal. You cannot fight an enemy you fear. It was to rescue us from the fear of death that God the Son became *a mortal* human being.

> The children of a family share the same flesh and blood; and so he too shared ours, so that through death he might break the power of him who had death at his command, that is the devil; and might liberate those who, through fear of death, had all their lifetime been in servitude. (Heb 2:14-15 NEB)

He shared your dying flesh that for you he might enter death, demolish the lord of death and build a wide firm bridge across it on which you might tread fearlessly.

He hell, in hell, laid low;
Made sin, he sin o'erthrew;
Bowed to the grave, destroyed it so;
And death, by dying, slew.

"As in Adam all men die," writes Paul, "so in Christ all will be brought to life. . . . Christ the firstfruits, and afterwards, at his coming, those who belong to Christ. Then comes the end, when he delivers up the kingdom to God the Father. . . . For he is destined to reign until God has put all enemies under his feet; and the last enemy to be abolished is death" (1 Cor 15:22-26 NEB).

Defeated, but not yet abolished. We will destroy it from the other side. Mortality will then have put on immortality, and you, like me, will wonder whatever it could have been that made us tremble before our last enemy.

You may conquer death now. Let its fear no longer haunt you. Look at the years that are left to you before death comes. What would you like to accomplish during that time, soldier? The Conqueror of death and hell has his arm around your shoulder. "It is I," he tells you, "Be not afraid. Look, I have armor for you. Let me buckle on your breastplate and show you how to use your sword. If you grip it firmly, your hand will shake less, and soon your fear will go altogether. Keep close to me. Though I am always in the thick of the fight, I'd rather have you near me than far away. Come follow me, soldier of mine. Follow me now."

As for me, John White, it is time for me to leave you. I wish I did not have to say goodbye. I would reach, if I could, through the paper to touch you. My longing is a selfish one. And though it springs from deep within me, I must not give way to it. Turn from me to Jesus your Conqueror. We may meet, you and I, on the battlefield or beyond it, but for the time it is imperative that we both fix our attention on Christ rather than on each other.

In the meantime I send you into battle with a prayer on my lips, a prayer that one day, you yourself will repeat the words of an old man, chained to a Roman soldier.

For I am now ready to be offered, and the time of my departure is at hand. I have fought a good fight, I have finished my course, I have kept the faith: Henceforth there is laid up for me a crown of righteousness, which the Lord, the righteous judge, shall give me at that day: and not to me only, but unto all them also that love his appearing. (2 Tim 4:6-8 KJV)

May it be so.

Notes

CHAPTER 3: GOD STILL SPEAKS
[1]Mary A. Lathbury, "Break Thou the Bread of Life."

CHAPTER 5: HIS INFERNAL MAJESTY
[1]Samuel W. Gandy, "I Hear the Accuser Roar."
[2]Ibid.
[3]Martin Luther, "A Mighty Fortress Is Our God."

CHAPTER 6: FAITH
[1]"How Firm a Foundation," in John Rippon's *Selection of Hymns*.

CHAPTER 9: HOLINESS
[1]J. C. Ryle, *Holiness* (London: James Clarke, 1956), p. 30.
[2]John Owen, "The Nature and Causes of Apostasy," in *The Works of John Owen* (London: Banner of Truth Trust, 1965), 7:26.

CHAPTER 10: DELIVERANCE FROM DRUDGERY
[1]Horatius Bonar, "Fill Thou My Life."

CHAPTER 11: THE FIGHT
[1]Charles Wesley, "Soldiers of Christ, Arise."
[2]Isaac Watts, "Am I a Soldier of the Cross."

IVP
CLASSICS

In today's information age, we are deluged with content but yearn for wisdom that will transcend the moment. IVP Classics are significant, compact books that have stood the test of time, written by trusted authors who have shaped the lives of millions.